BROKE TO BREAKTHROUGH

Harish Damodaran

'Chandramogan's business journey is a story for the ages. It should be studied at every business school in the world. Failure is not all bad; it reinforces what works and what doesn't. Chandramogan has never cut corners and always done what is right for producers and consumers. You can do right by both and still win. A message we can all believe in'—Laura Ries, global positioning guru and co-founder of Ries & Ries.

'*Broke to Breakthrough* is a story of frugality—the mother of all virtues—perseverance and a passion to keep climbing against various odds. It is also a story of innovation and striving to be different, be it in products or processes. Chandramogan's journey of taking a miniscule ice-candy business to becoming India's largest private dairy company is a beacon of hope for young entrepreneurs. Documented by one of India's finest agri-writers, I recommend it not only to those who wish to know about the sector, but also aspire to be something they are proud of'—Ashok Gulati, Infosys chair professor for Agriculture at Indian Council for Research on International Economic Relations (ICRIER).

'India's White Revolution is well-known, as the triumph of Verghese Kurien mobilizing farmer-based cooperatives and creating the legendary Amul brand. Harish Damodaran, arguably the most insightful reporter and writer on Indian agriculture, documents a counterpart dairy revolution in the private sector: R.G. Chandramogan using domestic risk capital sans any government support to incentivize farmers and creating the Arun ice cream and Arokya milk brands. A riveting tale of unleashing of Indian entrepreneurship and the harnessing of markets thanks to reform and liberalization'—Arvind Subramanian, former chief economic adviser, Government of India.

'Hatsun and its *atmanirbhar* founder's story is especially fascinating for aspiring entrepreneurs interested in built-to-last businesses. Chandramogan stands out for his shrewd commercial judgments, execution skills, persistent quest for excellence, personal integrity and sacrifice. He has time and again bucked conventional wisdom, relied on intuition and ensured not to repeat the same mistakes. India needs more Chandramogans in the agriculture sector to double, treble and quadruple farmers' incomes. May a hundred Hatsuns bloom!'—Gopal Srinivasan, managing director and chairman, TVS Capital Funds.

BROKE TO BREAK THROUGH

THE RISE OF INDIA'S LARGEST PRIVATE DAIRY COMPANY

HARISH DAMODARAN

PENGUIN
VIKING
An imprint of Penguin Random House

VIKING

USA | Canada | UK | Ireland | Australia
New Zealand | India | South Africa | China | Singapore

Viking is part of the Penguin Random House group of companies
whose addresses can be found at global.penguinrandomhouse.com

Published by Penguin Random House India Pvt. Ltd
4th Floor, Capital Tower 1, MG Road,
Gurugram 122 002, Haryana, India

Penguin
Random House
India

First published in Viking by Penguin Random House India 2021

Copyright © Harish Damodaran 2021

All rights reserved

10 9 8 7 6 5

The views and opinions expressed in this book are the author's own and the
facts are as reported by him which have been verified to the extent possible,
and the publishers are not in any way liable for the same.

ISBN 9780670095858

Typeset in Minion Pro by Manipal Technologies Limited, Manipal
Printed at Replika Press Pvt. Ltd, India

www.penguin.co.in

This is a legitimate digitally printed version of the book and therefore might not
have certain extra finishing on the cover.

To Neelambari and Charukeshi

Contents

Introduction

In 1970, when I started off as an ice candy manufacturer with a capital of Rs 13,000, three employees and fifteen pushcarts, there were probably 40,000 others all over India—3,000 in Tamil Nadu and 350 in Chennai—doing this business. My choice of industry at that point was guided not by any romantic entrepreneurial zeal, but the sheer need for survival. Mine was a cottage industry where everybody was a dwarf and largely stayed so—like bonsai trees, but not as beautiful.

I had the urge to grow, but was constrained by money, and had nobody to guide me or act as a torchbearer. I did manage to graduate from an ordinary stick-and-cup ice-candy to a genuine milk-based ice cream maker offering a range of varieties. However, my turnover in 1981 was just Rs 4.25 lakh. That was when I discovered my break-out formula. Those days the big ice cream brands focused only on city markets—in this case, Madras, as Chennai was then called. I decided to explore a new market that lay in the towns and urban centres outside of Chennai. It was an underserved market having several ice-candy but no good ice cream brands. Nobody had tapped into this aspirational consumer segment. We created an outstation market for ice cream and a new franchisee model of sit-and-eat parlours without our realizing it! By 1986, 'Arun' had become the market leader, not only in Tamil Nadu outside Chennai, but even in the capital city.

In July 1995, I ventured into liquid milk marketing. The underlying motivation, again, was survival. My annual sales from ice cream had by then reached Rs 11 crore. But I had invested in a Rs 2-crore plant for manufacturing instant milkshake powder, inspired by 'Rasna', the popular soft drink concentrate brand. My product bombed badly; its monthly losses of Rs 4–4.5 lakh were being funded through interest-free loans from the ice cream company. Around this time, I was advised by well-wishers to sell even my profitable ice cream business to Hindustan Lever, which had been acquiring one local brand after another. It was a tough choice between exiting and surviving.

Dairy, like ice cream, wasn't a sunrise industry. My entry, too, was only to recoup losses from a disastrous investment. Liquid milk sale was, moreover, a cooperative monopoly. Every state had a local cooperative that enjoyed government patronage and could run losses supposedly in public interest. That luxury wasn't available to entrepreneurs investing hard-earned capital.

The one lesson that I had learnt from 'Arun' ice cream was to take the untravelled road: my product, even if it was just milk, had to be different from my competitor's. The cooperatives mostly sold 'toned' milk containing 3 per cent fat and 8.5 per cent solids-not-fat (SNF). Rather than selling the same product at a lower price, I made a call to market only standardized cow milk with 4.5 per cent fat and 8.5 per cent SNF. My 'Arokya' milk would further be homogenized for better texture and uniform consistency. And like with 'Arun,' I promoted sales of 'Arokya'—as *naalarai paal* or 4.5 per cent fat milk—in Chennai as well as the big and small towns across Tamil Nadu. At the start of the century, my company, Hatsun Agro, was South India's biggest ice cream and private sector liquid milk player.

Today, when Hatsun has grown to a Rs 5,500 crore-plus turnover company and India's largest private dairy enterprise, I can list three major factors behind our success.

The first is being a change initiator and product differentiator. Ours wasn't a 'new' industry like IT, airlines, telecom or satellite television. Yet, that didn't stop us from doing new things even here, be it identifying and developing markets not on others' radar or creating niche products. *'Naalarai paal'* apart, we were the first to recognize the market potential of packed curd. Our target consumer was the working woman who had no time to set curd at home from milk. Curd is now my company's second highest revenue source—after milk and on par with ice cream!

The second is thrift and being focused on our business. I did embark upon a few misadventures and unrelated activities but exited in time and ensured these didn't affect my core ice cream and dairy operations. The profits from the latter were reinvested in their growth and never diverted towards accumulating land, gold and other personal assets. I take pride in staying in rented accommodations and not moving into my own home at Chennai until June 2000. No one can teach single-minded focus and commitment (in my case, to my business) better than Roger Federer. About ten years ago—this was at an exhibition tournament in Abu Dhabi, and I was there to watch my all-time favourite—the tennis legend was asked by a young boy what it would take to become the next Federer. Sacrifice was the answer he got. Federer told the lad that as a Swiss, he loved mountain-climbing but generally refrained from it as any injury could hamper his tennis career. Simply put, achieving excellence in any field demands sacrifice.

The third factor has been creating economic moats to gain competitive advantage and market share. We were never thrifty with regard to brand-building and investing in infrastructure, even if it meant borrowing from banks and our debt-equity ratio almost reaching 6:1 at one point. But all this risk-taking, to repeat, was for expansion within and not in unrelated businesses. Many of these investments—whether in procuring milk directly from farmers bypassing intermediaries, spending over Rs 100 crore every year on advertising and sales promotion or developing independent distribution franchisee networks—have taken time to yield returns. I believe we are at an inflexion point where these returns are really beginning to show. It is personally a great feeling that Hatsun Agro today directly touches the lives of some 4 lakh farmers, besides another 50,000 employees and trade associates. Two persons I would specifically credit for the company's growth, behind the actual execution of our business strategy from the mid-nineties, are K.S. Thanarajan and C. Sathyan.

A fourth factor, no less significant and in addition to the above three, is my grandmother Meenammal. Behind every successful person is a spiritual anchor, someone who always inspires and believes in you. Meenammal *mamamma* had faith in my future even when all others had given up. She has been my friend, philosopher and guide in good and bad times.

Last but not least, I am thankful to Harish Damodaran, who understands and writes on agriculture better than most in the country, for documenting the journey of Hatsun from its very start. His meticulous attention to detail prodded me to go back in time and recall people, things and events that were hidden in the deepest recesses of my mind. Without him, it would have been impossible to cover this voyage, which has had its share of failures and blunders as much as successes and accomplishments. I hope that Hatsun's story conveys to budding entrepreneurs the one lesson life has taught me: never lose heart and look for breakthroughs even when near broke.

R.G. Chandramogan

Foreword

'I started my business with an investment of Rs 13,000 and will think of exiting only when even that capital gets eroded!' This was the response given by R.G. Chandramogan to a suggestion that he sell out his company to a major multinational with deep pockets and a pan-India presence. That was in 1993 when its turnover was around Rs 9 crore. Today, nearly three decades later, Hatsun Agro Products' (HAP) annual sales exceed Rs 5,500 crore, and it has established itself as India's largest private sector dairy company.

I have heard a similar story about Harsh Mariwala, the owner-promoter of another Indian branded consumer products company, Marico. He was made a similar offer, perhaps not surprisingly, by the same multinational and also refused to succumb. The same goes for Karsanbhai Patel of Nirma. Taking on the challenge of big multinationals probably fires up the entrepreneurial energies in smaller players, leading them to innovate and create coalitions with their stakeholders that bigger companies don't consider worth the bother.

The broader policy lesson is that if we can create an environment that encourages competition and also provides support and succour to small and medium-sized firms, that have the fire in their belly to expand and take on everyone irrespective of reputation or size, India would see the rise of thousands of Karsanbhais, Chandramogans and Mariwalas. These 'Make in India' entrepreneurs will drive economic growth and generate large-scale employment necessary to meet the exploding aspirations of our young population.

Recounting the journey, from a precarious start to the present stature of being the country's biggest private dairy company, is surely a good way to celebrate the fiftieth anniversary of any enterprise. *Broke to Breakthrough,* authored by Harish Damodaran, does this most lucidly. Starting with a mere Rs 13,000, obtained from the sale of ancestral property, Chandramogan's is a proverbial rags-to-riches story. But with a major positive twist: its success has been achieved by constructing a corporate social enterprise that now takes care of over 4 lakh farmers and 50,000 employees, franchisees and vendors, while also supplying good-quality products to consumers.

Here is a major lesson for our young aspiring entrepreneurs: to gain market share and take on firmly entrenched competitors, an entrant firm has to build coalitions, which might seem costly in the short term but yields handsome returns in the long term. Having a long-term vision and pursuing it relentlessly, as Chandramogan has done and which is so well captured by the author, is the key to success. Short-termism, which is, unfortunately, becoming the common creed and egged on by the stock market's unreal expectations, does not create firms that can withstand competition from large dominant players and nurture global ambitions.

Chandramogan's company took roughly eighteen years to accomplish annual sales of Rs one crore (in 1987-88) and another thirteen years to cross Rs 100 crore. But the Rs 1,000 crore-plus mark was achieved in just the next eight years. That turnover doubled in the next four years and doubled again in the next four to reach Rs 4,000 crore by 2016–17. This implies an annual growth rate of about 20 per cent over the eight-year period when the national GDP was rising at less than 15 per cent annually in nominal terms. By 2019-20, HAP's turnover had crossed Rs 5,000 crore. The company's bounding growth reflects the almost insatiable consumption demand from India's ever-expanding middle class for products in which they see value for money. Here is, then, a lesson for those still waiting on the sidelines for investing in India: the country with its burgeoning domestic market holds out the opportunity to achieve global scale and high returns on investment. The upside potential is simply enormous.

HAP's and Chandramogan's story has multiple other insights on how to succeed in the Indian market. Hatsun grew with its consumers, first offering them real ice cream with 'Arun'. Later on, it introduced a high-end 'Ibaco' ice cream, so that its clientele, which had already tasted 'Arun,' did not escape to more established foreign brands. Another lesson is not cutting corners and being stingy on brand-building, as this is the key to capturing market share. Even while his company was relatively small, Chandramogan did not flinch from paying $30,000 for consulting a top-notch US brand expert. Not being scared of making mistakes, as long as one has the humility and courage to correct them in time and draw lessons, is another major learning from the Hatsun story.

For me, however, Chandramogan's concern for farmers, and his willingness to invest in their welfare and technological advance, is the most notable part of the story. His clarity on how to increase farm incomes is, indeed, impressive. 'The government wants to double farmers' income and guarantee them a minimum 50 per cent return over cost. We believe both are possible. But the right way to do it is not by hiking procurement prices year after year, which will only make Indian agriculture globally uncompetitive. Instead, it should be through bringing down the cost of production'. And he has proved that this can be done by taking the latest veterinary science and fodder development know how, including from the Tamil Nadu Agriculture University, to the dairy farms. This is the way forward for Indian agriculture, which needs a new paradigm to enhance the incomes of farmers, become globally competitive and, at the same time, work on the principles of agroecology to reduce its carbon footprint.

Such stories of successful Indian business persons should be multiplied manifold. People like Chandramogan have fought adversities and yet retained an ethical framework for their business operations while also improving the livelihoods of lakhs with them. Their experience would resonate strongly with budding Indian entrepreneurs who will easily identify themselves with the protagonists of these stories. This will greatly help in the emergence of true capitalism with Indian characteristics and a global footprint.

Dr Rajiv Kumar
Vice Chairman
NITI Aayog

Preface

My first book looked at capitalist enterprise in India, specifically from the standpoint of the social base of the country's business class and its expansion beyond traditional Vaishya mercantile communities. Since its publication in 2008, I was keen to do more detailed case studies or the micro-histories of individual entrepreneurs from diverse community and regional backgrounds. I had even begun work on a business biography of the founder of India's third largest industrial house at the time of Independence. But in the meantime, R.G. Chandramogan approached me to 'document' the journey of Hatsun Agro Product, the company he originally started as a partnership firm in 1970. Our conversation happened around early-August 2016.

There were many reasons why it didn't take me long to say yes. Foremost among them, of course, was my background as an agriculture writer and Hatsun being India's largest private dairy company. Chandramogan also caught my interest as a 'new capitalist'—a regional entrepreneur from a non-mainstream business community. But what made his company really worth documenting was its organic growth that traversed every potential stage of a business enterprise—from tiny to small, medium, big and, finally, large. And all through, Chandramogan has stuck to his knitting, starting with ice cream and then becoming an integrated dairy player, while not pursuing the usual 'conglomerate diversification' strategy of getting into unrelated businesses, be it real estate, infrastructure, finance or education.

Chandramogan has also struck me as different from other entrepreneurs in his obsession with having control over every facet of Hatsun's operations. This isn't 'control' in a negative sense, but manifesting itself in the company procuring milk directly from farmers (rather than bulk vendors, as most private dairies do), making everything (including the packaging film for milk and curd, chocolate paste and cones for ice cream, and renewable power for captive consumption) and compressing the distribution value chain (eliminating clearing and forwarding agents/super stockists).

Hatsun does not conform to the typical large Fast-Moving Consumer Goods (FMCG) firm, which would subcontract much of its manufacturing and even entrust distribution to sole-selling agents and other marketing intermediaries. Chandramogan's approach, instead, has been to invest in procurement, processing and distribution infrastructure, along with brand-building. All these have entailed incurring significant fixed overheads and variable expenses initially, but paying off with the costs getting spread over increased milk volumes and the company's products fetching a premium or selling faster on the strength of brand equity. Chandramogan's ability to reduce every expenditure or income into 'so many paise per litre of milk'—and doing these calculations in his head—is something that has always fascinated me!

Writing this book was relatively easy, being mainly based on interviews with Chandramogan and other directors and senior employees of his company. I must specially thank K.S. Thanarajan, C. Sathyan, H. Ramachandran, R. Premalatha,

J. Prasanna Venkatesh, A. Sam Joseph, John Henry Niezen, G. Reena Kamalarajan and A. Sundaravenkataraman, who were the most helpful in this regard. If the documentation took so long, it is testimony to Hatsun's own complex 50-years-plus journey.

This, as readers would see, hardly followed a straight and predictable pattern. The marketing, raw material sourcing and other organizational strategies, even for a company focused only on dairy products, have evolved over time. Such evolution—which is also a reflection of the capacity to innovate and adapt to changing situations—has, in fact, been key to success in its case.

There are four persons to whom I am particularly grateful for enabling me to finish this book and, hopefully, the other pending business biography project. Yamini Aiyar and Mekhala Krishnamurthy were very generous in providing me space and time at the Centre for Policy Research. Raj Kamal Jha and Unni Rajen Shanker, my editors at The *Indian Express*, were equally kind in allowing me to take a one-year sabbatical for the same. I cannot forget to thank Shreya Punj, and before her Anushree Kaushal, of Penguin Random House India for helping me to bring this book out. The credit for copy-editing and ironing out inconsistencies in the manuscript that I would ordinarily not have noticed goes solely to Shreya.

I hope that this book is useful for those interested in business and enterprise, whether from an academic or practical perspective. Firm histories are a mirror of not just the life, but also the times of the individuals behind them. They can shed light on economic matters that impersonal accounts of forces, pressures and policies driving change cannot do. There is a substantial corpus of literature on the Indian economy and business, both pre- and post-1991, but not much on individual firms and entrepreneurs that have been the products as well as prime movers of change. The last good firm history that I have read is of the engineering company Forbes Marshall called

The Rise of a Modern Parsi Enterprise by Ashok V. Desai. We need many more of them, especially of businesses built from scratch by people with meagre resources but vaulting ambitions and dogged perseverance.

Harish Damodaran

Note on Numbers and Spellings

Figures pertaining to sales, price or cost used in this book are mostly in rupees, paise, crore or lakh. One crore equals 10 million, while one lakh is 0.1 million, 100 paise is one rupee and one rupee is roughly 0.0135 US dollars at an average exchange rate of Rs 74 to the dollar in 2020.

The names of many cities or towns mentioned in this book have undergone change or modification over time. Thus, Madras is now Chennai, Bombay Mumbai, Bangalore Bengaluru, Calcutta Kolkata, Pondicherry Puducherry, Trichy Tiruchirappalli, Tuticorin Thoothukudi, Palghat Palakkad, Trichur Thrissur, Belgaum Belagavi and Gulbarga Kalaburagi. I have used the old and new names depending on the context and time for which the reference is made.

1

The Early Years

'*Thanni Thungam Mathiri. Oru chottum veenagakoodathu* (Water is like gold. Not a drop should be wasted).'

This was the first management lesson R.G. Chandramogan learnt and imbibed as a six-year-old venturing outside to play barefoot. The guru was his maternal grandmother Meenammal. She would give him just one jug of water for washing his feet before re-entering the home. The rule was well laid down: both feet were not to have a speck of dirt and cleaned using water from that single jug.

Water was a precious resource for the residents of Thiruthangal, a mofussil town in Sivakasi *taluka* of southern Tamil Nadu's (TN) Virudhunagar district, where Chandramogan was born on 1 March 1949 to a modest family of agriculturists. Thiruthangal was about 3 km from Sivakasi, 20 km each from Virudhunagar and Srivilliputhur, and 33 km from Rajapalayam. Apart from these were places like Vathirayiruppu (Watrap) and Ayan Vadamalapuram, just over 30 km and 45 km away, respectively. They all fell in a water-starved belt; Virudhunagar district's average annual rainfall of 799.8 mm during 1901–2000 stood well below India's 1,184.7 mm and even TN's 1,005.6 mm. Not for nothing, its black and red loam soil was traditionally suited only for dryland agriculture.

Yet, this belt would prove highly fertile for entrepreneurship, quite similar to Rajasthan's semi-arid Shekhawati region that gave rise to most of India's prominent Marwari industrial families—from the Birlas, Dalmias, Goenkas and Singhanias, to the Poddars and Piramals. The entrepreneurs from in and around Virudhunagar had more diverse community backgrounds: Nadar, Raju, Udayar, Naidu and Brahmin. And they made a mark by creating successful branded product businesses, both before and during Chandramogan's time.

Sivakasi is famous for three industries and names associated with them: safety matches ('Chavi' brand), firecrackers ('Standard' and 'Cock') and printing ('Nightingale' diaries and 'Lovely' cards). Virudhunagar has been a bustling trading centre for *dal* (pulses), oilseeds, chillies, coffee, cotton, rice and other farm produce. Its businessmen have also built brands such as 'Idhayam' sesame oil, 'VVD' coconut oil, 'Udhaiyam' *dal* and 'Kalimark Bovonto' aerated beverages. Rajapalayam is synonymous with the Ramco Group (Ramco Cements, Rajapalayam Mills and Ramaraju Surgical Cotton). It is also the hometown of the promoters of the Adyar Ananda Bhavan vegetarian restaurant chain. The founders of 'Pothys' textile showrooms and 'Pommys' women-wear come from Srivilliputhur, while the men behind 'Gold Winner' refined sunflower oil and 'Cycle' *agarbatti* incense sticks belong to Watrap. The legendary Dr Govindappa Venkataswamy, who started Aravind Eye Hospitals in 1976 after retiring as ophthalmology department head of the Madurai Medical College, was originally from Ayan Vadamalapuram.

Thiruthangal did not enjoy the entrepreneurial reputation of Sivakasi, Virudhunagar or Rajapalayam and was known more for its Ninra Narayana Perumal temple dedicated to Lord Vishnu.

The only notable business name prior to Chandramogan from this overgrown village—upgraded into a Town Panchayat in 1966 and made a Third Grade Municipality in 2004—was 'T.A.S. Rathinam Pattanam Podi', the snuff tobacco brand whose initials were short for Thiruthangal Ayyanadar Sabarathinam. But proximity to towns with vibrant commercial traditions helped, as some of that air was bound to percolate to Thiruthangal. According to Chandramogan, the remarkable thing about this whole belt is its entrepreneurs being a mix of locally based players and those establishing themselves in other places, like the Marwari desert diaspora. Also, they have created more brands than their counterparts from Coimbatore and other industrial hubs of the state.

Chandramogan's father, Raja K.S.P. Ganesan, being the only son, inherited 32 acres of land. It was, however, dry and barren, yielding crops such as cotton, groundnut and tapioca only in good rainfall years that were rare. Not surprisingly, the family—Chandramogan, too, was the only son of his father and mother, Sarkarai Thai, with two sisters, Indhumati and Kayalvizhi, both younger to him—led a precarious existence. When Chandramogan was eight, Ganesan, only 20 years older than him, migrated to Madras. He set up a small provision store at Rasappa Chetty Street in Park Town, barely a kilometre from the Madras Central railway station.

Chandramogan initially studied at a local school in Thiruthangal. On moving to Madras, he was admitted to the Bala Bharath School in Thyagaraya Nagar with a boarding facility. He studied there from Class IV to VIII, while securing a double promotion that allowed him to skip Class V. Living in a hostel, which had inmates from Andhra Pradesh, also helped him learn Telugu which would prove useful some years down the line. Chandramogan seemed to have been a reasonably good student until he joined the Muthialpet Higher Secondary School in George

Town, an institution founded way back in 1847, from Class IX. That was when he suddenly lost interest in studies, which had partly to do with his father's business not doing too well. Chandramogan could sense it and even expressed his keenness to join and help out.

'My father refused. He was keen that I went to the US, following the footsteps of one Shankaran, who was ten years senior to me and also from Thiruthangal. As a person, my father was very amiable and well-respected, especially by the people from our hometown who were mostly in the north Madras area and doing provision stores business. But as a businessman, he wasn't very astute. While his peers had a daily turnover of around Rs 1,000, my father's sales probably didn't exceed Rs 250,' recalls Chandramogan. Raja K.S.P. Ganesan served as the secretary of the Chennai Vazh Thiruthangal Hindu Nadar Uravinmurai Dharma Fund. Founded in 1956—its president was T.A.S. Chelliah, owner of the earlier-mentioned snuff concern—this was basically a charitable society of Thiruthangal Nadars living in Madras.

His father's business troubles clearly had an effect on Chandramogan, who failed Class X. He felt dejected but decided to repeat the same class and do it in English, rather than Tamil, medium. 'A couple of teachers made fun of me, pointing to my not clearing even in the regular Tamil medium. But I was somehow confident about doing well,' says Chandramogan. He was fortunate this time to have P.K. Srinivasan as his mathematics and English teacher. A founder of the Association of Mathematics Teachers of India in 1965, who also went on to be curator-director of the Ramanujan Museum & Math Education Centre at Madras, Srinivasan didn't believe in learning by rote. He wanted the students to learn to speak and write by themselves. When they did, he would correct them.

This approach of stimulating thinking and developing confidence in oneself appealed to Chandramogan. He would never forget the last day in school when Srinivasan addressed his students. 'If at all we meet some years from now, please do not introduce·yourself as a peon, stenographer or clerk whom I had once taught. I would consider that as an insult. Introduce yourself only if you are an engineer, doctor, lawyer, police officer, artist or a leader of your chosen profession,' were his words. The central message here was that one should aim for excellence in whatever line one chose to pursue. It was to make a lifelong impression on Chandramogan, who finally passed his Class XI (then, the School Leaving Certificate) with a first class. Moreover, he stood second in English from his school, despite having studied in Tamil medium previously!

If P.K. Srinivasan imparted self-belief and a sense of purpose and direction to the sixteen-year-old, the role models for Chandramogan when it came to a career goal were P. Ayya Nadar and A. Shanmuga Nadar. These two men had, in 1922 while in their late teens, set off from Sivakasi to Calcutta to learn about safety match making. Using that knowledge, they started matches manufacturing as a cottage industry back in their hometown. Within the next two decades, Sivakasi became India's 'Kutty Japan' (mini-Japan), with scores of units engaged in the manufacture of safety matches, followed by fireworks and printing, initially of trademark labels and posters. The effects of that revolution, unleashed in a barren, nondescript landscape like Sivakasi, were visible even in surrounding areas like Thiruthangal, where small production units had come up.

Chandramogan had grown up hearing about the exploits and riches of the early Sivakasi pioneers, including legends about their rivalry that extended to the Pongal Tamil New Year festival at the local Parasakthi Mariamman Temple. One popular story was of a competition in preparing the Pongal rice dish, where the fuel ostensibly used was not firewood but one-rupee notes. The one throwing more notes and whose rice cooked faster was the winner! The idea of becoming the next Ayya or Shanmuga Nadar—and from Thiruthangal—had appealed to Chandramogan right from as long as he could remember.

The urge to do business was even more after he had passed out of school. But Raja K.S.P. Ganesan was adamant about his son continuing to study and go to the US. Chandramogan was then sent to do his one-year pre-university course in science (physics, chemistry and mathematics) at the St Xavier's College in Palayamkottai, near Tirunelveli. He passed overall in first class but did not clear mathematics. This was the second time he had failed and was forced to repeat a year. In this case, his annual college and hostel fees also came to Rs 1,000. It could be paid only due to his father's mother, Vellayammal, who was managing the family's 32-acre farm at Thiruthangal. In 1966, one of those freak good agricultural years, she earned about Rs 20,000 from the sale of crops. That not only helped sponsor Chandramogan's education at Palayamkottai but also tide over a financial crisis from his father's losses in business.

By now, Chandramogan was tired of studying but had to enrol in a privately run Students Tutorial College at Madurai— yet again, at his father's insistence. In those days, repeating a year meant reappearing in the exams for all subjects, including those passed earlier. As it happened, on the day Chandramogan went to take his chemistry exam, he went completely blank. This was, strikingly, in a subject where he had done quite well. The exam started at two in the afternoon. Ten minutes on, he went straight to the hall-in-charge and expressed his disinterest in writing the exam. The invigilator was sympathetic and tried to dissuade the young man, though to no avail. All he could do was let him remain in the hall till 2.30 p.m., which was the minimum mandated time. At 2.35 p.m., Chandramogan got out of the examination hall at Madura College and went to a nearby theatre. There, he saw the Tamil film *Thangai* starring Sivaji Ganesan in the matinee show from 2.45 p.m. That over, he followed it up with

Maadi Veettu Mappilai, a Jayalalithaa-starrer, for the evening show from 6.30 p.m. to 9.30 p.m. That was in 1967, the year when both the movies were released.

The next morning, Chandramogan went to Thiruthangal, where his maternal grandfather Gurusamy Nadar and grandmother Meenammal—who had imparted him the precious lesson on thrift and managing scarce resources—lived. He was mentally stressed, and that was obvious to them. Gurusamy figured out that their grandson—he was a favourite of theirs—was in no mood to continue with studies. By then, he had also persuaded Chandramogan's father—who also happened to be Gurusamy's sister's son—to exit his struggling business in Madras. Gurusamy Nadar had a reasonably successful wholesale vegetable trading business in Thiruthangal. Given his advancing age, he felt that Ganesan could take it over. Gurusamy's own sons—Somasundaram, Shanmugasundaram, Soundarapandian and Sivanesapandian—were settled in Madras, where they had a textile showroom at Royapuram and a separate wholesale vegetable operation at the Kothawal Chavadi market near George Town.

For Chandramogan, this was a frustrating period. At the end of the day, he was a pre-university fail, whose doors for career advancement through education were practically shut. His ambition to pursue business, too, had met with stout resistance from his father. The latter refused to speak with him for six months after his abrupt move to discontinue studies.

This was where Gurusamy—who had previously been president of the Thiruthangal village panchayat—stepped in by putting in a word through his associates to Arumugaswami, a timber merchant in Villupuram, about 160 km south of Madras. Chandramogan joined as the junior-most among Arumugaswami's eight employees on a monthly salary of Rs 65 and stayed within his shop premises. He was least acquainted with the timber business but soon made an impression through his salesmanship.

His knowledge of both English and Telugu, which he had picked up during his Bala Bharath hostel days, was of help here. His ability to speak the latter language—more so, the chaste coastal Andhra version—appealed to customers belonging to the Reddiar and Naidu communities who were of Telugu origin. Besides, there were the more sophisticated buyers coming from not-too-far places like Pondicherry. They, too, were quite happy dealing with a young man comfortably conversing in English. In no time, Chandramogan got into the good books of many of these people, so much so that Arumugaswami sought his help in raising short-term loans from them.

'He wasn't very good at managing fund flows and often defaulted on payments. The customers whom I had befriended were willing to lend purely on my guarantee. I didn't want to lose that goodwill. So, I would arrange money from them for fifteen days and tell my owner that it was for seven days. On the sixth or seventh day, I would pressure him to return the money, which he, with his usual delay, did on the tenth or eleventh day. Thus, I ensured repayment before the fifteenth day, and both parties were happy,' recounts Chandramogan.

About nine months later, Arumugaswami put up a saw mill and entrusted its management to Chandramogan. Villupuram, then, had a sole mill sawing timber logs into planks and boards of various sizes. It belonged to a north Indian and was in the main town, whereas Arumugaswami's mill was in the outskirts on the Trichy road. The carts carrying the logs came from nearby villages into Villupuram either by the Trichy or Madras road. The new saw mill was in an isolated location, making it difficult to attract the carts heading to Villupuram. Chandramogan hit upon a strategy. He would get up early at around 3.30 a.m. to intercept the cart-men just before they entered the town by the Trichy road. A watchman was sent to do the same for the carts arriving by the Madras road a furlong away. They were further enticed to bring their logs to the saw mill, with the added sweetener of an early morning tea and straw for the bullocks. The plan clicked, and it did not take long for Arumugaswami's factory to become Villupuram's leading saw mill. Chandramogan, by now, was keen to go back to the original timber shop, as there was nothing to learn from being at the mill and dealing just with log carters. The owner wasn't willing. He wanted Chandramogan to continue at the saw mill. That was too much for a restless 20-year-old, who called it quits after about one-and-a-quarter years at Arumugaswami's establishment.

The only place he could go was Madras. His father had already moved to Thiruthangal, and the only ones still in Madras were his maternal uncles. By this time, Chandramogan's reputation was in tatters. He hadn't done well in his studies. Although he had displayed initiative and resourcefulness at the Villupuram timber shop and saw mill, his resignation in a huff wasn't viewed kindly. His uncles were accommodating nevertheless. He was offered the job of managing the cash counter at the textile showroom run by the two younger uncles, Soundarapandian and Sivanesapandian. But even there, he showed little interest. His mind was clearly bent upon starting something of his own. And it had to be different—not the usual provision store or textile retail business.

That was when the youngest uncle—Sivanesapandian was only five years elder to him—suggested that Chandramogan venture into ice cream making. He got the idea from an ice cream factory that one Lakshmanaswami had set up at Egmore that locally sold the brand called 'Mary'. Sivanesapandian felt that his nephew could open a similar operation catering to the Royapuram area. When Lakshmanaswami was approached, he didn't mind extending advice, as this was a business where only three brands had a pan-Madras presence: 'Dasaprakash,' 'Kwality' and 'Joy'. The bulk of the 350-odd players in Madras were small-time ice-candy manufacturers selling in local neighbourhoods within five or six kilometre radius. While Lakshmanaswami provided basic guidance on raw material sourcing, Chandramogan also met the owner of 'Rita' ice cream, a Punjabi gentleman by the name of Vijay Kumar Syal. 'He showed me his roughly 700 square feet facility at Royapettah. Again, there was no competition since his sales were primarily in the Triplicane and Marina Beach area, whereas the furthest I could have gone was to Parry's Corner (George Town),' remarks Chandramogan.

Chandramogan invested, in all, Rs 25,000 to establish an ice-candy unit on a 250 sq ft rented space belonging to his uncles adjacent to their showroom at Royapuram, apart from the purchase of twelve pushcarts and three tricycles for hawking the product. Out of the Rs 25,000, Rs 13,000 came from the sale of three small shops at Vilampatti, near Thiruthangal, that his father owned in addition to the family's 32-acre agricultural land. A loan from the Tamilnad Mercantile Bank financed the remaining Rs 12,000. Chandramogan's uncles arranged the loan and also stood as guarantors.

On 7 April 1970, Chandramogan's little factory, with a capacity to churn out 10,000 candies per day, began manufacturing and selling ice cream under the 'Arun' brand. It was set up through a partnership firm called Chandramohan Company, in which he and Raja K.S.P. Ganesan were the sole partners. It was only the start of what was to grow several folds within the next decade itself.

2

Growing with Ice cream

A 35 per cent net profit margin on sales is nothing short of a dream, for any business enterprise. For a new venture—start-up, in today's parlance—this kind of return would be pure magic. It was, indeed, so for a twenty-one-year-old's fledgling concern, which, in its very first year of operations in 1970–71, made a net profit of Rs 40,000 on sales of Rs 1.15 lakh. Chandramogan couldn't have asked for more!

Chandramogan's 10,000 candies-per-day plant comprised three production chambers, a five-litre batch freezer and five cold storage units, all procured from a local firm, Refrigerators & Home Appliances. The whole process involved first blending the raw materials—milk powder, cream, sugar and cocoa—in the chambers. This mix was fed to the batch freezer, which simultaneously churned and chilled it for about half an hour. Thus formed and already chilled to around 4 degrees Celsius, the ice cream was filled into cups or moulds to turn out sticks and bars. The resultant ice candies were finally taken to the cold stores and frozen to minus 18 degrees. Each such full cycle resulted in five litres of ice cream being produced and drawn into sticks, bars or cups.

During the peak summer period, Chandramogan clocked daily sales of Rs 550, of which Rs 300 was through pushcarts/tricycles and the remaining Rs 250 from a counter right in his factory premises facing the road. The ice cream making unit itself occupied only a 125 sq ft area, allowing the balance of 125 sq ft to be used as a retail outlet for walk-in consumers in a busy locality.

But success soon gave way to failure, which was an outcome of inadequate appreciation of what had contributed to the success in the first place. Chandramogan's profits were really coming from over-the-counter sales, on which there was no expense towards the supply of ice packs or commission to pushcart operators. The margins weren't as much in pushcart sales, where even getting vendors wasn't easy, especially in the busy summer season. Each operator sold some 200 sticks and eight to ten cups daily. These were at rates ranging from 10 paise for ordinary candies and 25 paise for juice bars, to 40 paise and 75 paise for cups and chocobars, respectively.

That was where Chandramogan made a blunder. Buoyed by the whopping success of his first year's performance, Chandramogan invested in an additional machine that was a more efficient one manufactured by Richardson & Cruddas. Further, he moved his existing production unit to a bigger 650 sq. ft premise rented for Rs 400 a month. This, he thought, would enable scaling up his operations for a product that seemed to be in great demand. The mistake, however, was in the choice of location.

The old factory was on the Gollavar Agraharam Road of Royapuram. While the new unit was only 200 metres away and more spacious, it was on the Singara Garden 8th Lane, behind the main road. The relatively inconspicuous location made it difficult to attract walk-in consumers, forcing greater reliance on the pushcart operators. These men, in turn, had the choice to hawk numerous ice-candy brands, with 'Arun' just one of them. In the second year, Chandramogan's turnover went up to Rs 1.50 lakh and peak season sales, too, rose to Rs 650–700 per day. But only about Rs 100 came through over-the-counter sales—that too, mainly from the old premises, on which he already incurred a monthly rent of Rs 250 plus the cost of employing an additional person. The remaining sales were from pushcarts (Rs 450) and party orders (Rs 100–150), on which the margins weren't much.

Worse, by May 1971, Chandramogan had also moved his parents to Madras. While earlier he worked and lived in the old factory premises, the family now stayed at a rented accommodation about 2 km away in Tondiarpet, costing Rs 200 per month. The rent of the newly hired premise, at Rs 400, was also higher than the Rs 250 for the earlier 250-sq ft space belonging to his uncles. Besides, there was the interest payable on a fresh loan of Rs 36,000 taken from the Tamilnad Mercantile Bank for the Rs 50,000 invested in the new factory set-up. 'Suddenly, my finances went awry. Although I wasn't running losses in the business per se, the overheads, including rents and other hitherto non-existent family expenses, suddenly mounted. On the other hand, sales weren't increasing commensurately, as it wasn't easy to push volumes from the expanded capacity through pushcarts, both in the peak season when the vendors acted pricey and in the off-season when they disappeared,' recalls Chandramogan.

Very soon, he was in the red and had to take help from his maternal uncles. During the three years from 1972 to 1974, his average outstanding loans to them were to the tune of Rs 40,000. The eldest uncle Somasundaram was particularly unhappy about this debt pile-up—on which no interest was being paid either—while demanding repayment as early as possible. Chandramogan felt guilty, even offering to sell his unit and using the proceeds to settle dues. Fortunately, the other three uncles were more accommodating. Soundarapandian told Chandramogan that if he were to sell, it would mean starting a new business and learning all over again. Instead, it was better to stick to what he was doing and work aggressively towards getting the existing business back on track. Those were very encouraging words.

Chandramogan, at this point, had very few options outside of pushcart sales. He had already shut down the old premises, from where sales over the counter took place but paying rent was no longer feasible. Selling through other retailers or departmental stores was possible, but that entailed supplying deep freezers, which he couldn't afford. Also, 'Arun' wasn't a brand like 'Joy,' 'Kwality' and 'Dasaprakash' that store owners would want to stock. The second option was to supply to big hotels and restaurants that served ice cream as a dessert item to customers. But they, too, insisted on the supply of deep freezers along with two months' credit for payments.

There was, however, one Ambi's Cafe at Broadway in the commercial centre of George Town that was willing to try out 'Arun' ice cream not for restaurant sales but its catering business. Shanmugasundaram, Chandramogan's second maternal uncle, knew its owners as he was a vegetable supplier to them. On his recommendation, Ambi's Cafe agreed to source ice cream from Chandramogan, provided though he upgraded the quality. That necessitated investing in a homogenizer and an improved manufacturing process using real milk, rather than powder, to make the mix. The mix had to be pasteurised (heat processing to kill pathogenic bacteria) and homogenized (breaking down the fat globules into smaller droplets to prevent their separation and rising to form a layer of cream at the top) and, then, taken to a vat. There, it was to be aged for 6–7 hours at about 4 degrees Celsius, which also allowed the fat to crystallize partially. This was followed by the adding of flavours and colours, churning and freezing, filling into cups/moulds, hardening, and final cold storage.

Chandramogan invested in a homogenizer—it was a second-hand machine costing Rs 7,500 and bought from a company called

Madhu Ice Cream in Agra, Uttar Pradesh—and hired a production manager by the name of Shankaran Kutty. The latter was looking for a job after working with Kwality, which had wound up its operations in Madras (the brand was to make a comeback later in 1980). Chandramogan offered him a monthly salary of Rs 400, not a small sum in 1972 and more so for a struggling business. But Chandramogan knew that without making the transition from an ordinary stick-and-cup ice-candy producer, to a homogenized ice cream maker offering a wider range of varieties with improved flavours, he couldn't hope to bag party orders through the likes of Ambi's. And that required getting someone having hands-on experience in ice cream production with an established brand.

Shankaran Kutty also told Chandramogan about a market that the big ice cream makers hadn't tapped: ship chandlers. Royapuram was just 5 km from the Madras port. The chandlers supplied the provisions to ships that called at the port, and Shankaran Kutty happened to know one of them wanting to source ice cream. This segment, unlike hotels or department stores, was fastidious only about quality and timely delivery. The brand did not matter, which was probably also why the established players did not target these buyers. The chandlers, moreover, didn't seek supply of deep-freezers, as the ships already had them. Chandramogan started supplying to one ship chandler and, in no time, got to know the others as well.

The other segment untapped by the established brands that Chandramogan identified was university and college hostels. The Indian Institute of Technology (IIT) Madras campus alone had eleven hostels, where ice cream was supplied as part of the menu once a week. The hostel food authorities included the mess secretaries, who were students themselves. Chandramogan had some inkling that they, too, would be flexible with regard to the brand and more interested in product quality along with timely, personalized service. Again, this segment did not excite the big players looking only at large orders or sales through regular retail store outlets. But for someone of Chandramogan's size, supplying small quantities was fine, as long as it promised regular weekly orders.

Chandramogan, in those days, used to travel by an Enfield Bullet motorcycle that he had purchased in 1974 for Rs 3,500. In the course of one of his rides through the IIT campus and making enquiries, which was followed by interactions with the mess authorities, he became a supplier to the hostels of the prestigious engineering institute. Soon, he was supplying to others as well, including the College of Engineering, Guindy, the Stanley Medical College at Royapuram and Ethiraj College for Women at Egmore. All these institutions were now also giving bulk orders for their annual days, attended by anywhere from 1,000 to 4,000 students along with parents while consuming one or two days of production at Chandramogan's factory. Depending on the college and the occasion, the orders could be for regular 70-ml cups costing 75 paise or even novelty cassata ball slices (which 'Arun' had introduced in 1972 itself) priced at Rs 2 each.

Towards the end of 1974, Chandramogan had captured 95 per cent of the Madras college hostels and ship chandlers segments, even though these represented only 5 per cent of the city's total ice cream market. In addition, he was supplying to Ambi's Café and Ashok Catering Services belonging to one Thomas Rajan. On 7 November 1973, Chandramogan supplied ice cream for the marriage function of Asokan Chakravarthy, whose family owned the 'Anandham' brand of sesame oil established by the latter's grandfather, V.V. Vanniaperumal Nadar, in 1942. Impressed by the product's quality, the family asked for it to be served at the reception that followed on 11 November at their hometown in Virudhunagar. It was the first-ever outstation order for 'Arun' ice cream, delivered at a location almost 500 km from Madras and served to over 1,000 guests.

By early 1975, Chandramogan's financial troubles were over, and he had managed to pay off his debts. In between, on 10 June 1973, he got married; the family of his wife Lalitha hailed from Tuticorin. From 1971 to 1974, Chandramogan also enrolled with Davar's College that used to offer short-duration programmes for management executives. He took courses in marketing and personnel management. 'I did it not for obtaining any certificates, but just out of interest and wanting to know. I even attended one session on export management and got introduced to terms like 'confirmed letter of credit without recourse'. None of these was of immediate relevance to my business,' notes Chandramogan.

Yet, at the back of his mind, there was this realization that the growth possibilities for 'Arun' within the existing segments were exhausted. He had, after everything, a 95 per cent-plus share in just 5 per cent of the Madras ice cream market. The remaining 95 per cent was virtually out of bounds for 'Arun'. In order to grow from here, he had to come out with something new—which could be by tapping yet another of those hitherto untapped segments.

The new segment this time—again unexploited by the overwhelmingly Madras-focussed dominant players—turned out to be outstation markets, starting with universities. In late 1974, Chandramogan got to know from a customer Ravindran about his nephew Selvam, who had taken a shine to 'Arun' ice cream while at Loyola College in Madras for about a month. He had registered there for a degree course before securing admission for engineering at the Annamalai University, where the product wasn't available. On making further enquiries, Chandramogan found out that the university had seven hostels. Ice cream wasn't part of their weekly menu, unlike in IIT Madras, but each of the seven hostels had their separate annual days that were pretty gala affairs. The annual days would start in mid-February and stretch up to mid-March, just before the close of the academic year, followed by examinations.

Sensing the latent potential in this market—which had dime a dozen ice candy, but no genuine ice cream brands—Chandramogan established contact with the hostel authorities and took a taxi in early-February 1975 to Annamalai University at Chidambaram, about 225 km south of Madras along the east coast. He also carried an ice-box containing samples of his product for the student secretaries of the hostels to see and taste. Predictably, it was well-liked. Chandramogan wasn't wrong in his assessment of the market potential either. In all, there were 13,000–14,000 students with relatives from the seven hostels present on different days of their annual functions over this period. Each consumed no less than a two-rupee cassata slice, translating into revenues upwards of Rs 25,000.

In 1977, Chandramohan Company had a turnover of Rs 2.75 lakh, out of which the seven days of Annamalai University sales alone accounted for close to Rs 30,000! Chandramogan was also supplying ice cream—packed in dry-ice (solid carbon dioxide) containers and transported from the factory by two-tonne vans—to the PSG educational institutions at Coimbatore and the A.V.C. College in Mayiladuthurai. But these weren't assured annual buyers like the Annamalai University hostels.

Side income

Shankaran Kutty was at the factory (he left in 1977, but had got a fellow Malayali by the name of Pavithran from Dasaprakash to replace him), an ex-ITC man, T.A. Adinarayanan, looked after sales, and his father Ganesan handled the cash counter ('Arun' was still being sold through pushcart vendors in the Royapuram area). With the ice cream business well-established and the day-to-day operations being taken care of by others, Chandramogan decided it was time to do something on the side to supplement the family income.

In September 1978, he spotted a classified advertisement in *The Hindu* from a manufacturer of plastic jerry cans. This company, Anupam Plastic Industries, wanted distribution agents in Madras. It happened to be that just around that time, V.V. Vanniaperumal & Sons, the same Virudhunagar-based sesame oil maker, had a requirement for 20-litre jerry cans. This was apart from the one-litre and five-litre cans in which its 'Anandham' oil was already being marketed. Sensing an opportunity, Chandramogan applied for an agency dealership.

A month later, the owner of Anupam Plastic Industries, one Mr Dubey, came to Madras and met Chandramogan, who told him that he could secure an order for 7,000 20-litre jerry cans. Dubey showed a sample of his product that seemed to be of acceptable quality. To begin with, he undertook to supply 1,000 cans, worth Rs 23,000 at Rs 23/can. Chandramogan went to Indore in Madhya Pradesh, where Dubey was based and gave him an advance of Rs 15,000 from V.V. Vanniaperumal & Sons. It was done in the presence of an acquaintance, who stood guarantee for delivery. Dubey produced the cans, which were not of the same quality as in the original sample. He was forced to take a price cut of Rs 3/can as a penalty. Chandramogan, then, ordered a second consignment of 1,000 cans, for which a fresh Rs 15,000 advance was made. Those cans did not even arrive within the promised time. A desperate Chandramogan rushed to Indore.

When Chandramogan had first met Dubey in Madras, the latter had claimed ownership of three cars and his plant having a capacity to manufacture 10 lakh cans annually. But this time in Indore, he discovered that Dubey, far from having three cars, had only a new Bajaj Chetak scooter—bought from the Rs 15,000 advance given for fulfilling the latest order! The plant also had a single machine in a barely 300 sq-ft area. Chandramogan's alert eyes saw that it took roughly three minutes to produce a can. Even if the plant operated twenty hours daily for 300 days of the year, it could, at best, churn out 1.2 lakh cans or a tenth of the claimed capacity.

An angry Chandramogan went straight to Dubey's acquaintance, who ran a pharmaceutical manufacturing operation, and told him that his friend was a fraud. The latter was impressed by how quickly Chandramogan had assessed the plant's actual capacity and admonished Dubey for tarring even his reputation as a guarantor. Dubey was eventually forced to sell the Bajaj Chetak scooter and use the proceeds to purchase the raw material (plastic granules) for producing the cans. Chandramogan stayed in Indore for a week and ensured that the cans were ready. The remaining 5,000 cans—out of the total 7,000 that the 'Anandham' sesame oil makers required—he sourced from National Plastic Industries Ltd in Bombay. The entire lot of 7,000 cans was delivered between December 1978 and February 1979, on which Chandramogan earned a 10 per cent commission amounting to over Rs 16,000.

The other agency job that Chandramogan took up almost simultaneously was with Khambete Kothari Cans. This one had some connection to his main business. Chandramogan was buying about 80 litres of milk daily for his ice cream factory from the Nilgiri Dairy Farm, which had an outlet near the Egmore railway station. This was being supplied in 40-litre aluminium cans manufactured by the Indian subsidiary of the Swedish engineering products firm Alfa Laval. Every morning, a tricycle rickshaw would go to the Nilgiri counter and bring milk to the Royapuram factory. In the evening, the same rickshaw had to travel the six-km distance to return the empty cans. Chandramogan found this cumbersome and tried to reason with the local Nilgiri Dairy staff on why the cans couldn't be returned the next morning when the rickshaw had to collect a fresh lot anyway; it would effectively save 12 km travel time both ways. But they refused, citing a shortage of aluminium cans. Alfa Laval, apparently, did not have the capacity to supply extra cans.

When Khambete Kothari Cans advertised for a dealership sometime in October 1978, Chandramogan was quick to respond. The company agreed to appoint him provided he first procured 100 aluminium cans costing Rs 25,000 at Rs 250 each. Chandramogan initially did not take up the offer. But in December, while in Indore settling his dispute with Dubey, he decided to take a bus to Khandwa further south in Madhya Pradesh. From there, he boarded a train to Jalgaon in Maharashtra, where Khambete Kothari had, only a year ago, invested Rs 75 lakh in erecting a 60-cans-per-day capacity factory at a five-acre industrial plot.

On reaching Jalgaon, Chandramogan met the company's managing director R.J. Kothari, and asked him if he could make a telephone call that could potentially generate an order. It was an unusual request, but Kothari agreed and booked a trunk call to Madras. The person at the other end, to whom Chandramogan spoke, was P.M. Natarajan, the brother-in-law of the Nilgiri Dairy Farm's owner M. Chenniappan. When Chandramogan enquired whether Nilgiri was interested in purchasing 60 aluminium cans, he got an affirmative answer. A stunned Kothari asked for Nilgiri Dairy Farm's central sales tax number, address and other details, all of which were furnished by Natarajan. The order being placed—it was worth Rs 16,800 at Rs 280 per can, inclusive of Chandramogan's commission of Rs 30—a delighted Kothari (he did not really show it) took his young visitor out for lunch. Khambete Kothari Cans had earlier approached Nilgiri Dairy Farm, but it did not result in any order only because the right people were not spoken to!

During the next five years, from 1979 to 1983, Chandramogan did a lot of aluminium can sales business, which ran side by side with his ice cream operations. 'I used to make 4–5 car trips a year, each 1,500–1,600 km, taking samples with me to show to buyers, mainly cooperative milk unions. I would start from Madras and go all the way to Kanyakumari and from there northwards through

Kerala before returning to Madras. Every year, I sold 3,000-odd cans, earning Rs 90,000. After deducting expenses (mainly on taxi, which used to be about 75 paise per km), I netted Rs 75,000, which took care of all my family expenses. So, whatever money that ice cream made could be ploughed back into that business, which ran independently,' recounts Chandramogan.

He also had a full family by now, with his daughter Deviga born in 1975 and son Sathyan following in 1978. The family, which included Chandramogan's parents, continued to maintain a simple lifestyle, living in their old rented two-bedroom, one-drawing room accommodation at Tondiarpet till 1983. Chandramogan bought his maiden car, a second-hand Ambassador costing Rs 32,000, in 1979. The family's first refrigerator came only in 1982. This happened after a friend visiting their home was offered only coffee when he wanted cold butter milk: 'He teased me that I sold ice cream and still didn't keep a fridge for myself!' This was only a manifestation of thrift, a value inculcated in him by his grandmother Meenammal. The meaning of 'thrift' in the Oxford Dictionary read as 'the habit of saving money and spending it carefully so that none is wasted'.

A new franchisee model

During this period, the ice cream business itself saw some new developments. In 1981, when Chandramohan Company's annual sales reached Rs 4.25 lakh—the aluminium can business was under a separate entity called Ganesh Corporation—Chandramogan moved his factory from Royapuram to a bigger 1,500 sq-ft space at Tollgate (New Washermanpet) in north Madras. Three years later, the plant shifted to an even larger 4,000 sq-ft adjacent plot, also rented, in the same industrial area. This one housed a bakery as well to produce cakes used in 'Arun' cassata slices previously being sourced from the Bosotto Bros bakery at Mount Road.

Chandramogan's family, too, now moved to a new rented house at Egmore to be closer to the Church Park Convent and Don Bosco School, where Deviga and Sathyan went. While the new plant was 14 km from his residence, Chandramogan had opened an office at Egmore itself to handle outstation sales.

Between 1983 and 1986, almost Rs 70 lakh was cumulatively invested in modernization and new equipment at the Tollgate factory. That included an imported German-make homogenizer from Brenn & Lube and a continuous freezer from Italy's Cattabriga to replace the old batch freezers. Besides, a new pasteurizer and mix preparation plant, along with a hardening tunnel (which prevents the growth of ice crystals and air bubbles, thereby giving the desired product texture), got installed. These were sourced from the Delhi-based Daffoo Engineering Enterprises. As a result, the total ice cream manufacturing capacity rose to 2,500 litres per day, from 200 litres prior to 1981. In 1986, Chandramohan Company was handling 1,000 litres of milk daily during the peak summer season, compared to 80 litres before 1981 and 15 litres back in 1972.

The above expansions followed a huge jump in 'Arun' ice cream sales. Chandramogan, we already know, was averse to supplying deep-freezers to retailers or offering them any material on credit. A standard 400-litre freezer in the mid-1970s cost some Rs 14,000, while the smaller 120-litre units came for Rs 6,000. The department store owners wanted these to be provided for free and the company to take responsibility for their maintenance. On top of it, they often used the same freezers to stock other products such as soft drinks and bottled water. Chandramogan wasn't going to be in this game.

Around early 1979, one Soundaravel approached Chandramogan expressing interest in setting up an 'Arun' ice cream parlour, for which he sought the supply of a deep-freezer. Chandramogan politely declined the request. A week later,

Soundaravel returned and this time conveyed that he would himself purchase a freezer. He had apparently been goaded into this by his wife Dhanalakshmi. On 19 April 1979, the first 'Arun' ice cream parlour came up at Mannarswamy Koil Street in Royapuram. Two more followed—the first at Tiruvottiyur High Road in the same Royapuram area and the other at Besant Nagar. In addition, a provision store in George Town and another at Tondiarpet started stocking 'Arun' ice cream in freezers bought by the owners themselves.

Soundaravel's outlet made sales of Rs 450 on the opening day and continued to do Rs 250 daily for the rest of the year. Its location, on the main Royapuram road, also reminded Chandramogan of the blunder he had committed eight years ago in moving his unit from Gollavar Agraharam Road. Like Soundaravel, he could well have established a proper 'Arun' ice cream parlour there! All the five outlets in Madras were set up between 1979 and 1981. But the actual sales growth was to take place only with the opening of outstation parlours.

On 14 April 1981, a tyre dealer in Madurai by the name of Kanagaraj—he happened to be the brother of Soundaravel's wife Dhanalakshmi—invested in a deep-freezer and started a 'sit-and-eat' Arun ice cream parlour near the Vaigai river bridge of the temple-town. It turned out to be a resounding success. In 1983, when Chandramohan Company's turnover hit Rs 13 lakh, Rs 3 lakh came from just Kanagaraj's parlour: It did business worth Rs 4 lakh that year, of which Rs 1 lakh was Kanagaraj's own dealership income. 'I give full credit to Dhanalakshmi. She was the one who got both her husband and brother to overcome their initial reluctance and put money in the parlour and deep-freezer infrastructure, which I couldn't myself have done,' admits Chandramogan.

Seeing the success of Kanagaraj's parlour, many more such small-town agents felt encouraged to open such 'sit-and-eat' Arun ice cream outlets by investing in their own deep-freezers. Between 1981 and 1983, these outlets came up at Kumbakonam, Trichy, Pondicherry, Vellore, Dindigul, Theni, Virudhunagar, Sivakasi, Tuticorin, Tirunelveli, Kanyakumari, Coimbatore and Erode—practically every town in Tamil Nadu with a population of above one lakh. Ice cream from the Tollgate plant was despatched to these centres by regular fast passenger trains in steel trunks with double walls having thermocol insulation and dry ice slabs stuffed in between. The trunks were loaded from the Madras Central and Egmore railway stations at night while reaching the different destinations the following day between around 6.30 a.m. and 10.30 a.m. The outlet owners who had cleared the consignments would later book back the empty boxes on the same returning trains.

Two things were at work in the creation of a state-wide parlour network within such a short period. The first had to do with ice cream being a novelty item in most of the above upcountry towns. They had many ice-candy makers or hotels/restaurants serving home-made, unbranded, plain-vanilla ice cream, but nothing more. 'Arun,' by contrast, was good-quality ice cream available in cups, bars, chocobars, cassata, cakes and other formats and flavours. Moreover, it was an aspirational product; Chandramogan made 'Ice cream supplied from Madras' a key selling point in the advertisement banners and hoardings for 'Arun' in these centres. It was another matter that 'Arun' hardly sold much within Madras. But the fact that none of the big brands was present in the upcountry markets—they did not think there was a sizable aspirational consumer segment here waiting to be tapped—made Chandramogan's job easier.

The second aspect related to the unique franchisee model that Chandramogan had evolved, without his consciously realizing it. The 'sit-and-eat' outlet owners were, for all practical purposes, franchisees that had invested in their own parlours and deep-freezers. Chandramogan offered 'Arun' dealerships not to big businessmen or established traders but to young individuals with average family background and only the drive to do well. Once appointed, the franchisees were assured of exclusivity: there would be no other 'Arun' ice cream outlets in their vicinity. The product would further not be distributed through any other channel, barring direct deliveries to customers against specific bulk orders for marriages and parties. But as part of the exclusivity deal, the franchisees were not given material on credit. While the industry norm for payment was two months, in this case, it had to be made within two days of taking delivery. Not being stuck with receivables freed up resources that could now be invested in brand building and capital expenditures within the factory.

Capital entry

Having captured virtually 100 per cent of the market for genuine milk-based ice cream in TN outside of Madras, Chandramogan set his eyes on the capital city that was still a bastion of 'Dasaprakash,' 'Kwality' and 'Joy'. In overall volume sales, 'Arun' was already number 2 in the state behind 'Dasaprakash' by 1982 but had very little presence in Madras. In November 1982, Chandramogan suffered a jaundice episode that incapacitated him for three months. That was when he decided to exit the agency sales business for Khambete Kothari Cans to concentrate full-time on ice cream.

In 1983, 'Arun' was introduced into the city market as a pan-Madras brand. The television era had just begun. Even though there was only a single state-owned broadcaster, Doordarshan, the absence of too many channels helped in mounting a focussed advertisement campaign. Ramya Krishnan, who was still a few years away from attaining stardom—her acting career had barely taken off—was roped in to promote 'Arun' ice cream. Chandramogan did not engage any big ad agency either. But the

30-second commercials that were aired on Doordarshan created quite a splash: the catch lines included *Kuzhanthaigal party galata, Arun Ice Cream tarume cassata* (Make your children's party a gala affair by serving 'Arun' cassata) and *Virundinar vandal upacharam, Arun Ice Cream samayathil upaharam* (If you want to welcome guests, give them a gift of 'Arun' ice cream).

Creating a splash was central to the aggressive campaign to establish the 'Arun' ice cream as a brand in the challenging Madras city market. In 1985, a two-wheeler 'slow race'—the winner being the one who drove the slowest—was organized at the Egmore police parade ground. 'It attracted a crowd of around 4,000. They were mostly the young and upwardly-mobile type, who owned a motorbike or scooter, and the target consumers for our product,' observes Chandramogan.

On 28 August 1988, an 'Eat All You Can' Ice cream Mela was held at the Guild of Service hall, again at Egmore. This was a fair where anybody could enter, paying Rs 8, and eat any amount of ice cream on display in 20 minutes. Once again, over 4,000 landed up, with many more waiting outside the venue. The aim was to get people to try out higher-end flavours, which they would ordinarily have avoided experimenting with. In this case, only ice cream costing more than Rs 5—the likes of cassata, choco crunch and Italian Delight—was offered. The average participant ended up having ice cream worth about Rs 36 at the maximum retail price. 'We wanted to upgrade the consumer, exposing him to premium quality ice cream, unlike our competitors who were offering plain vanilla or strawberry,' says Chandramogan, who was to organize two more slow two-wheeler races in 1989 and January 1990. The last one, held in Bangalore, had the cricketer Javagal Srinath as the chief guest. He, like Ramya Krishnan, wasn't quite a star yet; his international career was to be launched only in late-1991.

Along with brand promotion, a franchisee network was also developed. The lead was taken by one Avadi Ganesan, who was named after a suburb in Madras where he resided. In 1984, he started a franchisee outlet in Avadi. Over the next couple of years, he got some fifteen others, basically relatives and friends, to also open parlours. By 1986, there were forty-five such exclusive 'Arun' ice cream outlets in Madras. During that year, Chandramohan Company's sales zoomed to Rs 29.52 lakh, and 'Arun' became the city's number 1 ice cream brand.

On 4 March 1986, Chandramogan incorporated Hatsun Foods Private Limited. On 30 April that year, Chandramohan Company was dissolved and all its assets vested with the new entity. The new name reflected a more modern corporate identity and also consistent with its market leader status. 'I was initially considering Hot Sun, given the association of ice cream with summer, but that was too direct. I eventually settled for Hatsun, which was close and yet different. And it sounded good,' recounts Chandramogan.

In 1986, Chandramogan also met P.K. Srinivasan, his old schoolteacher. 'If at all we meet some years from now, please do not introduce yourself as a peon, stenographer or clerk whom I had taught once'—those words, from somebody who was all through a source of inspiration, he hadn't forgotten. 'Now that I had achieved something, I felt a sudden urge to meet him and introduce myself. I managed to track him down. He didn't remember me but asked what I was doing. At that point, I mentioned what he had told our last class about twenty-one years ago. He was delighted to know that the company I built had become a market leader,' says Chandramogan, who remained in touch with his Guru till he passed away on 20 June 2005. In the late-1980s, he financed the publication of two popular books, *Number Fun with A Calendar* and *Romping in Numberland*, authored by this very committed and original mathematics teacher.

Hatsun Foods' turnover touched Rs 98 lakh during the financial year that ended on 31 March 1987. Three years later, it had further almost tripled to Rs 2.78 crore. With a network of 170 franchisees all over TN, 80 in Madras alone, the company had left its once-formidable competitors far behind. This was achieved not only by focussing on brand promotion and quality, but also by making sure that the product was always available to consumers: during a diesel shortage incident in 1987-88, 'Arun' ice cream was delivered on horse-carriages! Around that time, a 'Hatsun Privilege Card' scheme was also introduced. The said card was issued to anyone buying Rs 40 worth of ice cream, entitling the person to a 10 per cent discount on additional purchases from any 'Arun' parlour.

The success story of Chandramogan's company could be attributed to it overturning the established rules of the game. The old rules said that ice cream was a product mainly for big-city consumers. Hatsun showed that there was a market for good-quality ice cream even in small towns. It was previously believed that ice cream could only be sold through retailers and provision stores, who had to be given deep-freezers free of cost along with two months' credit on material supplied. But here was a company that had evolved a unique franchisee model of parlours exclusively selling 'Arun' ice cream, with the owners finding it worthwhile to invest in the deep-freezers and other outlet infrastructure themselves. Nor did the company extend any credit. Having applied the new rules to small-town markets successfully, it did not take long for Hatsun to use these to break into the Madras city citadel and become *numero uno* there as well.

3

From Ice cream to Dairy

At the start of the 1990s, Hatsun Foods was Tamil Nadu's undisputed market leader in ice cream. Its Tollgate factory had an ice cream manufacturing capacity of 3,000 litres per day and could handle 1,500 litres of milk daily in the peak summer months. But the existing facility was proving inadequate to supply the growing demand. With no space for housing a dedicated cold storage, the entire ice cream produced was actually being kept in deep freezers within the factory. All this imposed constraints on expanding production—there was literally no space to grow—while making it increasingly difficult to service markets from Madras in the north down to Nagercoil in the deep south.

Chandramogan initially toyed with the idea of looking for land within Madras to build a new factory. But given the challenges of securing government permissions and congestion in the city, not to speak of higher land or rental costs, the plan was given up. Around September 1990, he decided to purchase land in Salem. During his travels for the sale of aluminium cans, Chandramogan had noted that Salem, along with Erode and Coimbatore, was part of TN's main milk belt. The latter two districts were, however, further westwards. Salem's central location made it closer to major markets outside Madras, including Trichy, Madurai or even Coimbatore and surrounding areas. Salem was also only about 200 km from Bangalore and within 300 km of towns such as Palghat and Trichur in Kerala.

'It made sense to use the Tollgate plant to produce ice cream mainly for Madras. And since about 55 per cent of our sales were happening outside Madras, the Salem unit could service this as well as new markets like Karnataka and Kerala,' recalls Chandramogan, who was in a hurry to have the new factory up and running before the peak consumption season in April-June 1991. T.A. Adinarayanan, the sales head at Hatsun Foods, was sent to identify an appropriate location in Salem. A 2.5-acre plot was eventually bought at Ramalingapuram on the main Salem–Madras highway and registered by October 1990. With the same 3,000 litres/day capacity, the factory was commissioned on 19 March 1991, well in time to catch the ice cream season.

'It was a success from day one because the brand and market for the product had already been created. So, there was no problem in selling whatever got produced,' notes Chandramogan. The land for the Ramalingapuram unit was purchased at Rs 1.65 lakh per acre, a tenth of what it would have cost in Madras. Besides, there were roughly 18 per cent savings in raw milk costs. For the Tollgate factory, Hatsun Foods was sourcing pasteurized milk from Nilgiri Dairy Farm at around Rs 7.5/litre which was delivered at its gate. At Ramalingapuram, it could be procured fresh from local bulk vendors or even directly from farmers at a factory gate price of just over Rs 6/litre. The savings were basically in transport—Nilgiri Dairy was getting milk from Erode—and processor's margins that added up to 18 per cent. Employee cost, too, was lower in Salem compared to Madras. Above all was the location advantage, in terms of reaching markets outside of Madras. There was no need to even dispatch by rail now.

The total investment in the Ramalingapuram ice cream plant—covering land, building, plant and machinery—was in the region of Rs 52 lakh. Chandramogan personally put in Rs 15 lakh, with the rest financed through a loan from the Tamilnad Mercantile Bank (Rs 23 lakh) and borrowings from friends and associates (Rs 14 lakh). The factory was set up under M/s. Atlantic Foods, a separate sole proprietary concern of Chandramogan. The reason for it had to do with ice cream manufacturing being reserved for small-scale industries (SSI). The investment limit in plant and machinery to qualify as an SSI unit was Rs 60 lakh. Even the Tollgate unit was under a separate partnership concern called M/s. Hatsun Foods Company. Both, in turn, supplied their entire ice cream production to Hatsun Foods Private Limited.

By 1994–95, the annual sales of 'Arun' ice cream from the Tollgate and Ramalingapuram plants had touched 23.34 lakh litres valued at Rs 10.97 crore. This was up from their respective levels of 14.5 lakh litres and Rs 4.79 crore for the financial year ending on 31 March 1992. The total number of franchisees had crossed 400, and the brand was selling even outside TN—mainly in and around Bangalore and in cities of Kerala, especially Calicut, Quilon and Trivandrum.

In April 1995, the Tollgate unit was closed down, and the ice cream manufacturing operations shifted about 20 km further northwards to a place called Nallur in Ponneri *taluka* of Thiruvallur district. This was a brand new factory on a 3.5-acre plot, entailing an investment of Rs 3.5 crore, including in land, building, plant and machinery, and a cold room. The refrigerant used in the Nallur facility was ammonia. It was more economical and enabled large-scale production compared to freon that was being used in the Tollgate as well as Ramalingapuram factories. 'Our volumes were increasing, so we needed a bigger plant. Much of the funds for Nallur came from reinvested earnings, which was possible because our margins (profit before depreciation, interest and tax) on sales were 15 per cent or so,' says Chandramogan. The Nallur plant had an ice cream manufacturing capacity of 8,500 litres per day. The Ramalingapuram factory's capacity, too, had been expanded to 6,500 litres. The two plants together could produce 15,000 litres of ice cream per day and handle 7,500 litres of milk in the peak season. The milk for the Nallur factory was entirely procured from farmers, while in Ramalingapuram, half was from farmers and the balance from bulk vendors.

No more carts!

By the end of 1995, when Nallur was up and running, all the sales of ice cream through push carts were stopped. According to Chandramogan, the total 'Arun' pushcart/tricycle numbers never exceeded the initial fifteen, and once the franchisee route had established itself, 'we did not bother to replace the ageing operators who were gradually dropping out'.

Among them was S.M. Prakash, an 'Arun' ice cream pushcart vendor till about 1971 and thereafter a tricycle operator for another fifteen years. During those days, he delivered the product from the Tollgate factory to Ashok Leyland's commercial vehicle manufacturing facility at Ennore, around 12 km away, in the morning. After returning in the afternoon, he would ride the tricycle again to the IIT campus that was another 21 km. On the whole, it meant covering a daily distance of some 66 km. The need for such backbreaking labour fell as franchisee sales picked up alongside increasing delivery through vans. Also, pushcart/tricycle sales weren't the most desirable way to promote what was, after all, a premium ice cream brand. Prakash was re-engaged as a packer-cum-deliverer of ice cream in vans. Later, when the ice cream factory moved to Nallur, he joined as an employee in Hatsun's packing division and worked till his retirement on turning sixty in 2010.

Near fatal

Meanwhile, even as the ice cream business was doing well, Chandramogan committed what was to prove a mistake, quite like the decision over two decades ago to move his fledgling candy-making unit just 200 metres away from Gollavar Agraharam Road. On 29 July 1992, Chandramogan incorporated Hatsun Dairy Private Limited. This was a new company manufacturing instant milkshake powder under the brand called 'Santosa,' whose literal meaning was happiness. A sum of Rs 2 crore was invested in a plant on 3.5 acres of land in Karumapuram, hardly 3 km from the Ramalingapuram ice cream facility. The plant could process 10,000 litres of milk per day and convert this into one tonne of powder. The inspiration for it was 'Rasna,' the popular soft drink concentrate brand owned by the Ahmedabad-based Pioma Industries. Chandramogan thought he could replicate Rasna's success with a product that was milk-based and healthier. The New Delhi-based Ashish Technical Services was engaged as the turnkey contractor, with SSP Private Ltd at Faridabad near the national capital, supplying the machinery.

'Santosa,' however, failed to live up to its name. Unlike 'Rasna,' which was a simple concentrate where one needed to merely add water, the 'Santosa' powder had to be churned in a mixer grinder along with ice in order to create the milkshake. The idea of churning ice in a mixie did not appeal to homemakers, who thought it would damage the blades. The product bombed. 'Far from becoming a national brand like Rasna, which was my original expectation, it couldn't even cross TN borders,' concedes Chandramogan, who had personally invested Rs 1.2 crore and mobilized Rs 80 lakh as equity contribution from acquaintances.

There was another reason for the product's failure. The peak season for milkshake powder sales—the summer months from April to June—was when milk supplies were also low. On the other hand, when availability rose during the flush season, there wasn't much demand for the product. To deal with this problem, the company started manufacturing and selling ordinary milk powder as well. But commodity milk powder had to be produced at a lower cost because the realization from it was only about Rs 28 per kg, as against Rs 20 for a 200 gram packet of instant milkshake powder.

Moreover, the Karumapuram plant's capacity of one tonne per day did not offer the requisite economies of scale. It was viable only so long as a relatively high-value item was being manufactured. And that product simply did not click.

The new venture—renamed Hatsun Milk Products Limited on 8 March 1994—was a flop from day one. The company's sales grew from Rs 55.89 lakh in 1993–94 to Rs 1.70 crore in 1994–95, Rs 5.09 crore in 1995–96 and Rs 15.18 crore in 1996–97. But it made losses after tax in each of these financial years (April–March): Rs 49.95 lakh, Rs 55 lakh, Rs 45.55 lakh and Rs 30.43 lakh, respectively. All through this, the ice cream business—Hatsun Foods Private Limited, too, was renamed Hatsun Milk Food Ltd on 9 August 1995—continued to make money. But there was a limit to its supporting a bleeding venture.

Between 1994–95 and 1996–97, the ice cream company gave interest-free loans totalling Rs 2.42 crore to Hatsun Milk Products. The more the cross-subsidy and incomes foregone, the more undermined were 'Arun' ice cream's own growth possibilities. At stake also was the interest of the people—apart from Chandramogan—who had put in Rs 80 lakh as equity in the hope of some return.

Out of the Rs 80 lakh external equity contribution, Rs 30 lakh came from the family of K.S. Thanarajan, who had studied with Chandramogan at St. Xavier's College in Palayamkottai and gone on to do a master's in Economics from St. Joseph's College at Trichy. After passing out in 1972 with a first class and fifth rank at Madras University, Thanarajan worked for a year in Canara

Bank and from 1974 to 1980 in Southern Petrochemical Industries
Corporation's Tuticorin unit. He left the company as a deputy
manager of finance to join his family's business in Virudhunagar.
They were into moneylending and cardamom trading. The 1950-
born Thanarajan was the youngest among fourteen siblings. His
eldest brother K.S. Periyasamy was twenty-five years senior to him.
Another brother Selvarajan used to go for auctions at cardamom
trading centres like Vandanmedu and Kumily in Kerala's Idukki
district. One of his sisters, Jagadambal, was married to V.V.
Vanniaperumal's son V.V.V. Rajendran, who, in 1986, launched
his own 'Idhayam' sesame oil brand that eventually outsold
'Anandham'.

'We used to bid on behalf of buyers in Bombay, Delhi, Calcutta
and Kanpur, besides bringing the material to Virudhunagar and
grading it before despatching to these places on a consignment
basis,' informs Thanarajan, who was asked to take over the
cardamom trading operations after Selvarajan suffered a heart
attack. The family's primary income, however, came from lending
money at 27 per cent per annum or thereabouts to cardamom and
coffee planters or small-scale units in Sivakasi. The Rs 30 lakh in
Hatsun Dairy was their first-ever equity exposure, that too, in an
unrelated field. It was mainly courtesy of Thanarajan's another
sister's son A. Chandrasekaran, who happened to be of the same
age and had been with him (and Chandramogan) at St. Xavier's
College. Chandrasekaran—who was a supplier of roots, herbs and
other raw materials to ayurvedic drug makers—had independently
put in Rs 6.25 lakh in the new venture, which acted as a spur to
Thanarajan's family committing Rs 30 lakh.

Hatsun Dairy started on 19 May 1993. Thanarajan joined
as a director in the company on 5 October the very same year.
'Between 1993 and 1995, we lost Rs 4–4.5 lakh every month. It was
a harrowing experience,' recollects Thanarajan. This was also the
time when Hindustan Lever had entered the ice cream business,

acquiring one local brand after the other. Among those to sell out was 'Kwality,' which was doing a turnover of Rs 4 crore in Madras. Rajiv Khanna, the owner of the brand in the city, got Rs 9 crore from the Indian subsidiary of the Anglo-Dutch multinational. He advised Chandramogan also to follow suit. 'I was myself doing a turnover of Rs 9 crore then, but his whole point was that it wouldn't be easy to take on somebody the size of Lever, with deep pockets. My answer was simple: I started my business with an investment of Rs 13,000 and would think of exiting only when even that capital was eroded!' states Chandramogan.

In late-1994, Chandramogan and Thanarajan went to Nagpur, where they met Jimmy Rana, the owner of Dinshaw's Dairy Foods Private Limited. Rana was known to Chandramogan through a common friend Rajni Shah, a Bombay-based supplier of ice cream paper cups. Dinshaw's was, at that time, selling 25 per cent more ice cream than Hatsun and had also ventured into liquid milk processing and marketing. It was marketing 80,000 litres per day of milk filled in sachets in Nagpur city. Rana was the one who recommended that Hatsun enter into liquid milk sales as an alternative to the loss-making powder operations. He introduced Chandramogan and Thanarajan to Dilip Sarda, an Ahmedabad-based consultant who had earlier worked with the National Dairy Development Board and the ice cream maker Vadilal Industries.

Milky Way

Liquid milk marketing those days was a cooperative monopoly. TN used to have several private players, but they were all small and mostly selling 9,000–10,000 litres per day each. The biggest of them, Nilgiri Dairy Farm, did 40,000-50,000 litres, of which 30,000-odd litres was actually in Bangalore, another 5,000 litres in and around Erode, and only 10,000 litres in Madras. The bulk of their sales, moreover, were to hotels, tea shops and other wholesale buyers. The total volume handled by private dairies was a fraction of the 13 lakh litres or so daily procurement and sales of the Tamil Nadu Co-operative Milk Producers' Federation. Much of its 'Aavin' brand sales comprised toned milk containing 3 per cent fat and 8.5 per cent solids-not-fat (SNF).

Chandramogan had decided that if Hatsun was to get into liquid milk marketing, it had to do something different. The company wasn't going to sell the same toned milk at a lower price than 'Aavin,' to begin with. Nor would it deliver milk in cans to wholesale consumers, as most private dairies were doing. Instead, it would only supply branded milk in retail pouches to households. This milk was to also contain extra fat and be sold at a higher rate, as a value-for-money offering similar to 'Arun' ice cream. Thus, if 'Aavin' toned milk was priced at Rs 8 per litre, Hatsun would sell standardized milk with 4.5 per cent fat and SNF of 8.5 per cent for Rs 9 a litre.

Furthermore, the milk sold under Hatsun's 'Arokya' brand—the Tamil word for health—was to be homogenized, the suggestion for which came from Dilip Sarda. Homogenization was a process for breaking the fat globules into smaller droplets so that they stayed suspended uniformly in the milk, rather than rising to the top and forming a layer of cream. Homogenized milk had a better texture and uniform consistency that was also good for curd-making. And with the 1.5 percentage points extra fat, Chandramogan was sure that the housewife wouldn't mind paying a rupee more. While others within the company, Thanarajan included, weren't so sure, Chandramogan's opinion was the one that prevailed.

By early 1995, Hatsun Milk Products Limited—as the dairy company was called—had obtained an MMPO (Milk and Milk Product Order, 1992) registration from the Central Government to process up to 80,000 litres per day of milk. With Sarda's help, the Karumapuram plant was modified so that it could process and package liquid milk. The existing powder factory had chilling and pasteurizing facilities. All that needed to be added was a homogenizer, pouch packing machine and cold storage. On 10 July 1995, the company launched its 'Arokya' brand of homogenized, standardized milk in Salem. As an initial concession, Chandramogan allowed it to be retailed at the Rs 8-per-litre rate of 'Aavin' non-homogenized toned milk. But this was only for a period of three months, after which it was raised to Rs 9 per litre.

Sales of 'Arokya' milk stood at 1,800 litres on the first day. By December 1995, the company had launched it in Coimbatore. Over the next six months, other towns near Coimbatore and Salem— Tiruppur, Erode, Perundurai, Attur and Namakkal—and also Chennai (as Madras was now called) were covered. In 1995–96, milk sales averaged 14,148 litres per day, reaching 22,000 litres by March. Average daily liquid milk sales more than doubled to 30,992 litres in 1996–97 and further to 68,707 litres the following fiscal year. By 1997–98, Hatsun Milk Products Limited had turned around, posting a profit after tax of Rs 2.11 crore on sales of Rs 31.17 crore. This was as opposed to a loss of Rs 30.43 lakh on sales of Rs 15.18 crore the previous fiscal year.

Meanwhile, Chandramogan had come out with a public issue for Hatsun Milk Food Limited, the company that was marketing the ice cream from both the Ramalingapuram and Nallur plants. The issue, made in January 1996, involved an offer of 18 lakh fresh equity shares of Rs 10 each at a premium of Rs 35 and for listing at the Madras, Bombay and Coimbatore stock exchanges. The company succeeded in mobilizing the targeted Rs 8.1 crore from the sale of the 18 lakh shares making up 36 per cent of the post-issue paid-up capital of Rs 5 crore. While the initial objective was to raise money for expansion of the ice cream business— there were plans to open a new factory at Belgaum in northern Karnataka—it was becoming clear that the Hatsun group's future lay essentially in milk.

In 1995–96 and 1996–97, sales of 'Arun' ice cream, at Rs 13.85 crore and Rs 18.41 crore, respectively, exceeded the corresponding Rs 5.09 crore and Rs 15.18 crore for 'Arokya' milk. In 1997–98, it was the reverse, with the sale of 'Arokya' milk, at Rs 31.17 crore, surpassing the Rs 21.27 crore from 'Arun' ice cream. 'Ice cream was giving us the margins, but not turnover. Milk had the turnover, even if not margins. The growth in the future could only come from milk, but it also called for huge investments that would pay over time,' points out Chandramogan. Towards mid-1996, around 9 acres of land had been purchased at Belgaum with the intention to put up an ice cream plant for servicing new markets, including Maharashtra and right up to Bombay (now Mumbai). That plan, however, was shelved within a year's time.

On 1 April 1998, Hatsun Milk Products Limited ('Arokya') was merged with Hatsun Milk Food Limited ('Arun'). It was also decided to rechristen the latter as Hatsun Agro Product Limited (HAP), which would have both dairy and ice cream marketing operations under a single entity. For the financial year ending on 31 March 1999, HAP recorded a profit after tax of Rs 2.07 crore on sales of Rs 79.99 crore. Out of this, Rs 45.33 crore was from milk and Rs 24.25 crore from ice cream. The balance of Rs 10.41 crore was mainly from the sale of *dal* or split pulses—*tur* (pigeon-pea) and *urad* (black gram)—under the 'Apurva' brand. This was yet another misadventure and unnecessary diversification that Chandramogan had embarked upon in early-1998, emboldened by the turnaround in the dairy business. He was wise enough to shut down the *dal* division in less than two years' time. From now on, Hatsun Agro was to be only in dairy and ice cream, with the focus more on the former. This, despite ice cream no longer being an item reserved for SSI manufacturing, a restriction that the Union government had removed in April 1997.

As 'Arokya' milk sales continued to grow, reaching an average of 92,082 litres per day in 1998–99, the company had to secure an increase in the Karumapuram plant's MMPO-registered capacity, first to 130,000 litres in 1998 and then to 300,000 litres with effect from March 2000. Getting the approval wasn't an easy task. The dairy industry was technically de-licenced after July 1991, but the cooperatives had managed to use the MMPO as a weapon to create entry barriers. Under it, any dairy plant processing more than 10,000 litres per day had to seek registration from the state government concerned. In the event of the capacity exceeding 75,000 litres, the registration authority was the Central government. In both cases, the registration certificate was granted only if the appropriate authority was satisfied that the area ('milk shed') where the new or additional capacity was proposed had surplus milk. Further, it required a no-objection from the state milk commissioner, who often doubled up as the managing director of the cooperative dairy federation.

Chandramogan remembers how he struggled to obtain the approval, particularly for the expansion of the Karumapuram dairy's capacity to 300,000 litres per day. TN's daily milk production, then, was about 117 lakh litres, out of which roughly 68 lakh litres was the surplus available for processing. As against that, the existing processing capacities registered under MMPO in the state added up to not even 35 lakh litres per day, including 28.5 lakh of cooperatives and 6.5 lakh of private dairies. Moreover, barring Hatsun, the dairies weren't even using their registered capacities; the milk procurement by all district unions affiliated to 'Aavin' averaged less than 16 lakh litres per day in 2000–01.

In spite of that, the state government's representative, at the meeting of the MMPO central registration authority in New Delhi in February 2000, stubbornly maintained that there was no surplus milk in HAP's milk shed area. Thankfully, his objections were overruled by N.K. Sinha, secretary to the Government of India in the Department of Animal Husbandry & Dairying.

'He understood our point. But for him, we would have run the risk of procuring beyond our registered capacity. That would have technically been a crime even if we were procuring directly from farmers and they were benefiting from competition to buy their milk,' remarks Chandramogan.

The MMPO restrictions—nothing but licencing reintroduced through the backdoor—were eventually lifted in the Union Budget of 2002–03. It did away with the concept of 'milk shed'. Henceforth, the MMPO's remit was limited only to enforcement of prescribed standards in relation to sanitation, hygiene, quality, and food safety. Setting up new or expanding existing processing capacity ceased to be a crime. 'Liberalization in the dairy sector truly arrived only in 2002, not July 1991. Though the policy bias against private dairies continued, it was significantly alleviated by the amendment to the MMPO on 26 March 2002,' emphasizes Chandramogan.

In 1999–2000, sales of 'Arokya' milk averaged 138,526 litres per day. The following year, it hit 217,644 litres, even as HAP crossed a major landmark: for the year ended 31 March 2001, the company's sales touched Rs 149.83 crore with profits after tax of Rs 2.61 crore. These numbers for the previous fiscal stood at Rs 97.05 crore and Rs 98.99 lakh, respectively. Out of the total sales of Rs 149.83 crore, Rs 114.71 crore was from milk, Rs 32.13 crore from ice cream and Rs 2.17 crore from other dairy products. That included *khoa* and cooking butter under a different 'Dairy Choice' brand.

While the transformation to a dairy company was complete, 'Arun' ice cream retained its market leader status in Tamil Nadu. Between 1994–95 and 2000–01, sale volumes grew from 23.34 lakh to 37.58 lakh litres, even as the total franchisee base more than doubled from 400 to 943. In the meantime, the ice cream plant at Ramalingapuram was shut in July 1999 and the entire production shifted to the Nallur facility. Since the SSI reservation for ice cream manufacturing was gone, it made little sense to have two separate factories. The proprietary concern Atlantic Foods was wound up, and it was decided to have only production of *khoa* and butter at the Ramalingapuram site. Also, M/s. Hatsun Foods Company, the other concern through which the manufacture of ice cream was being undertaken at Nallur, was merged with HAP by 2003–04 in order to ensure more synergy of operations under a single roof.

But there was no doubt that liquid milk marketing was what had become the thrust area receiving the management's maximum attention. At one level, this was a serendipitous development. Till 1994, liquid milk wasn't even on Chandramogan's radar. He had entered the segment only to recoup losses from a disastrous investment and keep the Karumapuram operation going. The plant needed to produce something to be able to run in the flush season when milk supplies were abundant, but there was no demand for the product (shake powder) being manufactured till then. However, from nowhere and within no time, 'Arokya' milk had emerged as HAP's mainstay brand.

By 2000–01, some seventy clearing and forwarding agents and 2,500 retailers were pushing just 'Arokya' milk sales. Like in the case of 'Arun,' this product was being offered solely against cash on delivery. The distributors and retailers, in fact, did not even mind paying a deposit against two days of supply, simply because the product was fast-moving. The 1.5 percentage points extra fat in 'Arokya' standardized milk made it a value proposition for consumers over the regular toned milk. Besides, it was homogenized while being marketed as milk that was wholesome and healthy.

In October 1999, HAP became India's first dairy to spend Rs 1.25 crore for installing a 'bactofuge' machine at its plant. Bactofugation went one step ahead of normal pasteurization, which entailed heating the milk to around 75 degrees Celsius for fifteen seconds using continuous-flow process heat exchangers. It killed over 90 per cent of the bacteria, especially the disease-causing harmful pathogens such as *Mycobacterium bovis* and *Salmonellae*. Pasteurization, however, left out certain heat-resistant bacteria and spores (seeds) that could break down the milk proteins and cause curdling. Bactofugation was a non-thermal process for removing all bacteria, including the heat-resistant spores, using a high-speed centrifugal separator. The bactofuge employed the principle of expelling the bacterial spores (which are heavier than milk) through centrifugal force action.

In early 2002, HAP got Radhikaa, the well-known actress and star of the popular prime time Tamil serial *Chithi* aired on Sun TV, to endorse 'Arokya' milk. The fact that the serial was based on the theme of women's empowerment—with Radhikaa portraying the role of a strong and assertive character—lent further credibility to the brand.

Expansion mode

During this period, there were two other notable developments. The first was the commissioning of HAP's second dairy plant at Desur in Belgaum on 27 August 2000. As earlier noted, the land for this was originally meant for an ice cream factory catering to new markets in northern Karnataka and Maharashtra, including Mumbai. But seeing the growth in 'Arokya' sales, it was decided to install a 75,000 litres per day capacity dairy. In its first year of operations, the Belgaum dairy sold 25,000 litres daily on an average. The philosophy was the same. The cooperatives under the Karnataka Milk Federation procured and marketed milk under the 'Nandini' brand mainly in the southern districts of Kolar, Bangalore, Tumkur, Hassan, Mandya and Mysore. Borrowing from 'Arun' ice cream's experience, Chandramogan knew it wasn't worthwhile trying to offer more of the same (toned milk) in existing markets. Instead, it was better to sell standardized milk in relatively virgin market towns such as Belgaum, Hubli-Dharwad, Bijapur, Gulbarga and even Goa. Procuring an MMPO registration for a dairy was also easier in a belt where the coops had little presence.

The second development was the acquisition by HAP of Ajith Dairy Industries Limited (ADIL), which had a 100,000 litre per day plant at Thimmasamudram in Kanchipuram, barely 75 km from Chennai. In 1999–2000, this company did average sales of 88,000 litres per day of toned milk, half of it in bulk loose form and the rest in pouches under the 'Komatha' (cow mother) brand.

There were two attractions to its being a good buy. The first was location. HAP marketed around 50,000 litres daily of 'Arokya' milk in Chennai, which was being transported from the Karumapuram dairy over 320 km away. ADIL's plant was not even one-fourth of that distance. Secondly, the plant was in the advanced stage of obtaining an MMPO approval for increasing its registered milk handling capacity to 175,000 litres per day. With the dairy sector still under License Raj—unlike other industries in the post-reform era—there couldn't have been a more compelling rationale for taking over this unit. ADIL, moreover, wasn't a loss-making concern. For the financial year ending on 31 March 2000, the company had posted a profit after tax of Rs 74.75 lakh on net sales of Rs 39.23 crore. The dairy was reasonably well-managed, thanks to its vice president (production & technical) V. Iyappan.

ADIL's problems had to do with its promoter P.G. Saranyan, who had floated a 'Nidhi'—a mutual benefit non-banking financial company—by the name of R.P.S. Benefit Fund Limited. This company had collected deposits from members and failed to discharge the repayment amounts on maturity. Saranyan had allegedly siphoned off part of the monies to promote ADIL, in which he and two other co-directors had an 81 per cent stake. The balance of 19 per cent was held by R.P.S. Benefit. Subsequent to

R.P.S defaulting on payments to the tune of Rs 42 crore to 13,000 depositors, a criminal case was registered. The Madras High Court superseded ADIL's management and appointed an administrator to take charge of its affairs in March 2000. The court also ordered the sale of the promoters' stake in ADIL to part-pay the Nidhi's depositors.

HAP bought the 81 per cent stake of ADIL's promoters through a court-mediated auction and took over the company management from the administrator in the third week of October. The deal entailed a cost of Rs 10.5 crore, at least Rs 2.5 crore more than what a greenfield plant of similar size would have. 'Erection of the Belgaum dairy, which was of almost the same capacity, cost me Rs 7 crore. Even after factoring in more expensive land closer to Chennai, this one should have fallen under Rs 8 crore. The extra money was basically the Licence Raj premium for a plant about to get an MMPO registration for 175,000 litres,' states Chandramogan. HAP further had to clear Rs 2.9 crore of ADIL's working capital and term loans owed to the State Bank of India.

In all, the investment in the Belgaum and ADIL facilities, plus expansion of the Karumapuram dairy, worked out to over Rs 22 crore and within a short space of time. Much of this was financed through an ICICI Bank loan of Rs 16.5 crore, which also went towards settling ADIL's liabilities and prepaying the Industrial Development Bank of India that had initially extended assistance to expand the Karumapuram plant. 'Even after availing these loans and investing from our internal accruals, we fell short by about Rs one crore. The gap had to be filled by borrowing from a Sindhi financier at 18 per cent annual interest for three months. Looking back, we had undertaken a reckless expansion in our pursuit to grow the liquid milk business. The resultant interest charges were to put a heavy strain on our resources,' concedes Chandramogan.

The bridge loan from the Sindhi gentleman was a story in itself: 'He had dealings with ADIL's previous owner (Saranyan) and demanded 24 per cent interest, but I negotiated a lower rate. The Rs one crore actually came from 225 clients who had accounts with him. I had to sign promissory notes along with three-month post-dated cheques for an average sum of Rs 50,000 against each of their names. After clearing the loan at the end of three months, I asked him how he had given money with no security other than the promissory notes and cheques. He then narrated a tale told by his grandfather of a moneylender who was approached by a person for a Rs one-lakh loan. It was to start a new business after he had lost everything. When security was demanded, the man pulled out a hair from his moustache, which the moneylender promptly took as collateral and extended the loan. Weeks later, another person came and sought a Rs 2 lakh loan, against which he offered two moustache hairs as security. The moneylender refused this time. His logic was straight. What the first man had pledged was his prestige. A person with self-esteem will always return to reclaim lost glory, whereas the second man had pledged mere hair devoid of any real value. The Sindhi financier basically had belief in my personal integrity and commitment, which for him was good enough as security'.

By the end of 2000–01, the Hatsun Group was controlling three dairies, selling an average 300,000 litres daily of 'Arokya' standardized and 'Komatha' toned liquid milk. This was in addition to the nearly 38 lakh litres per year of 'Arun' ice cream that retained its market leadership in TN even after Hindustan Lever's entry through 'Kwality Wall's'.

Consumer to Farmer

Both liquid milk and ice cream were consumer-facing businesses. They called for significant investments in brand promotion and maintaining an extensive network of retailers and exclusive franchisees. But on the other side were the suppliers of HAP's primary raw material: milk. By 2000–01, there were 24,659 farmers pouring milk directly to the company, accounting for a significant share of its average daily procurement of 2.85 lakh litres in TN.

For Chandramogan, direct procurement—producer-facing, in other words—wasn't social service but a sound business strategy. Even as early as 1988, the then Tollgate ice cream factory had started buying milk directly from farmers, first through a centre opened at Ponneri (collecting eighteen litres per day) and then at Periyapalayam (120 litres) on the outskirts of Chennai. In 1990, a third centre was started at Gummidipoondi, procuring 280 litres daily.

According to Thanarajan, the Karumapuram dairy was procuring around 6,800 litres of milk per day when he joined Hatsun in October 1993. Out of this, only 2,600 litres or so was via bulk vendors at the Vellalagundam Cross Road about 15 km from the plant. The remaining 4,200 litres was already being sourced directly from farmers through two routes plied by separate vehicles. The first one was on the Agrahara Nattamangalam route, which had twelve centres buying a total of 2,400 litres. The second was on the Valapady route covering nine centres and purchasing 1,800 litres. At Puthiragoundampalayam village of Salem's Peddanaickenpalayam taluka, the first collection centre was on the Valapady route.

Each centre involved an investment of Rs 10,000 to hire a place and give six months' advance rent, provide tables and chairs, and keep aluminium cans and lab equipment/chemicals for testing of fat and SNF. Besides, the centre-in-charge had to be paid a salary. However, Chandramogan was convinced that the investments would pay off by securing milk supplies. These tended to go up during the flush season when the demand for ice cream as well as milk shake powder—the Karumapuram plant's original product—was low. On the other hand, the demand for the same products rose during the summer, which was also the lean season for milk supplies. During that period, the bulk vendors, too, would push up prices. Once Hatsun got into liquid milk marketing, Chandramogan realized the importance of stable round-the-year raw material supply—which only direct procurement from farmers could guarantee. 'Those days, the cooperatives used to not pay for three to four months. We made sure that the farmer's payment was made in cash once every ten days, and there was no default on this count. While he got a better price, the landed cost of milk still worked out lower for us, as we had eliminated an intermediary layer,' explains Chandramogan.

Interestingly, at the time HAP toyed with the idea of direct procurement, there was divergent opinion within the company on it. Prasanna Kumar Menta, production manager at the Ramalingapuram ice cream unit who previously worked with 'Dasaprakash', was used to transacting with bulk vendors. But P. Selvaraj, a procurement officer who had just joined from 'Aavin,' was keen to adopt the cooperative model of buying directly from farmers. Chandramogan opted for the latter model, though more as a commercially prudent strategy. Hatsun, for him, was in the business of liquid milk marketing, and that necessitated looking beyond the immediate. Building long-term relationships with suppliers—in this case, farmers—had to be integral to any sustainable business model.

By 2000–01, 82 per cent of the milk for the Karumapuram dairy was being directly procured from farmers and only the remaining through bulk vendors. In the just taken-over Thimmasamudram and the new Belgaum plants, the bulk vendor share was 100 per cent. In the course of the next fifteen years, HAP's procurement operations were to be 100 per cent producing-facing, something that no private sector dairy—barring Nestle at Moga in Punjab—had done or even attempted before.

On the personal front, Chandramogan moved into his own home in June 2000 at Akkarai in Chennai's East Coast Road. All these years, between 1973 and 2000, he had stayed in five rented accommodations. Only in June 2000—by then, he was fifty-one years old—could Chandramogan lay claim to a truly settled existence! Prior to that, in 1997, he got his daughter married. Chandramogan's son, Sathyan did his Bachelor of Business Management from Brisbane in Australia after passing out from Don Bosco School. Upon returning in 1998, he worked for a year as an apprentice with Fichtner, a Swedish engineering consultancy firm in Chennai. Sathyan joined Hatsun in 1999, where he was initially posted as an administrative officer in Salem studying milk procurement and production operations at the plants there. After about a year, he moved to HAP's Chennai office and was inducted into its board as executive director (operations) in June 2001.

While Chandramogan may have taken an inordinately long time to build a home of his own, he had the satisfaction of already having built an institution that would outlast him. And Hatsun still had a long way to go, despite having a turnover of Rs 190 crore in 2000–01 along with ADIL.

4

Challenges amidst Growth

The first half of the opening decade of the new century marked a period of significant growth for HAP. Between 1999–2000 and 2004–05, the company's net sales shot up from Rs 97.05 crore to Rs 449.19 crore. While annual sales of ice cream rose from 28.73 lakh litres to 41.61 lakh litres, the real increase was in liquid milk—from an average 1.39 lakh litres per day (LLPD) to 7.87 LLPD. Hatsun was also now South India's biggest private dairy concern, ahead of the Hyderabad-based Heritage Foods (which, until 1999–2000, before HAP's acquiring Ajith Dairy, had a higher turnover) and others such as Tirumala Milk Products, Dodla Dairy and Creamline Dairy Products. They had all emerged during the nineties, following the de-licencing of the dairy industry.

But growth came at a cost. As of 31 March 2000, HAP's aggregate debt, at Rs 10.86 crore, was well below its equity (share capital plus reserves) of Rs 15.94 crore. Five years later, this had reversed. The company's secured and unsecured loans now stood at Rs 90.75 crore, almost four times the shareholders' funds of Rs 23.01 crore.

The borrowings were largely for undertaking capital investments. By 2004–05, HAP's ice cream plant at Nallur (also called Red Hills) could produce 25,000 litres per day, while the company's total installed milk handling capacity was nearly 15 LLPD, as against 2.5 LLPD in 1999–2000. The Thimmasamudram unit—taken over from Ajith Dairy, merged with HAP effective from April 2001—had a liquid milk processing capacity of 2.5 LLPD, with these at 3 LLPD and 1.5 LLPD, respectively, for the Karumapuram and Belgaum plants. By September 2003, the Thimmasamudram dairy had a milk powder plant as well of 10 tonnes per day capacity (equivalent to 1.2 LLPD of milk). A bigger powder factory of 25 tonnes per day (3 LLPD of milk equivalent) was commissioned at Karumapuram in December 2004. In the second half of 2004, there was also a separate facility for concentration of one LLPD of milk at Thimmasamudram (normal milk contains about 12.5 per cent solids; that proportion can go up to 40 per cent in concentrated milk, allowing more quantity in terms of solids to be transported within the same tanker space). On top of these were two more liquid milk processing plants of one LLPD-plus capacity each at Bangalore and Kolkata, both taken on lease and operational from July 2003 and March 2004, respectively.

All these entailed heavy outlays. The Timmasamudram powder plant built by Alfa Laval cost Rs 6.5 crore. The same firm also constructed the Karumapuram facility. Its cost was Rs 30 crore, due to the higher capacity and also being more energy-efficient and state-of-the-art. Further, HAP was paying monthly lease charges of Rs 7 lakh and Rs 13 lakh for the Bangalore and Kolkata plants belonging to Balan Natural Food (of one A. Nanda Kumar) and Delight Dairy Ltd (promoted by Raj Kumar Agarwal), respectively.

'Financing these investments through debt made sense when we were hardly borrowing otherwise. Since farmers got payment for milk only after ten days, it effectively meant obtaining raw material on credit. At the same, the strength of our brands allowed us to demand immediate payment from distributors and retailers. With no material supplied on credit and everything being cash-and-carry, there were no issues of trade receivables. We were, thus, practically operating on negative working capital and borrowing only to invest in fresh milk processing and procurement infrastructure. Besides, we spent on brand promotion, advertising and marketing, which for us was also an investment for future growth,' notes Chandramogan.

However, some of the investments—shelling out about Rs 27 lakh to acquire the Kolkata dairy's 'Delight' brand, in addition to paying the monthly lease charges—were made more on impulse. 'We had expanded too fast. The idea was to use the Kolkata dairy to gain a foothold in other markets, including Jamshedpur and the North-east. Even before that, the Belgaum plant was supplying milk to Pune, some 340 km away, while we were sending concentrated milk produced at the Thimmasamudram powder plant to Dinshaw's Dairy at Nagpur. The concentrated milk facility that came up independent of the powder plant in late-2004 was supposed to cater both to Kolkata and institutional buyers such as Dinshaw's,' explains Chandramogan. The plans came a cropper, as the anticipated volumes didn't materialize. In Bangalore and Kolkata—where the company was marketing milk under the 'Hatsun' and 'Delight' brands, respectively—sales could barely reach 25,000–30,000 LPD each, thereby not justifying the monthly lease payments.

Inability to achieve volumes had earlier contributed to the failure of a couple of other products, too. That included sweetened *khoa*—milk concentrated up to one-fifth of its original volume—which HAP launched in 2000 under the 'Dairy Choice' brand. *Khoa* was used as an ingredient in a wide variety of Indian sweets. There were places such as Srivilliputhur in Virudhunagar district famous for their *khoa* (*palkova*, in local parlance) makers. HAP started manufacturing the same product from its shut ice cream plant at Ramalingapuram for sale to sweet-makers in Chennai, Bangalore and other towns. But the volumes turned out too small for a company of its size. Also, unlike pouch liquid milk and ice cream, khoa wasn't a directly consumer-facing product and nor could HAP compete with unorganized players supplying to buyers not really fastidious about quality. 'Dairy Choice' *khoa* had to be withdrawn within a year. A similar fate befell 'Noosa,' a branded popcorn launched in September 2000 for dispensing through microwave ovens installed at 'Arun' ice cream parlours. That one, too, bombed.

'I had made mistakes when my business wasn't all that big. I continued doing so even after it had grown. The important thing was to learn the right lessons from mistakes and make sure one didn't keep repeating them,' remarks Chandramogan on a philosophical note. The chickens nearly came home to roost in January–March 2004. That was a quarter when HAP incurred an operating loss of Rs 3.38 crore, even without factoring in interest outgo and provision for depreciation. It was like going back to the 1993–96 days of the bleeding Karumapuram instant milk shake powder venture.

'Many things happened together. The Belgaum dairy was losing money, as building markets in north Karnataka took time, and we were forced to sell in places such as Pune. In the same January–March quarter, Dinshaw's stopped taking the 40,000 litres-per-day of milk that we were supplying in concentrated form. Moreover, the Karumapuram powder plant and the dedicated milk concentration facility at Thimmasamudram were still under construction. We were, then, sending about 1.25 LLPD of surplus milk to dairies in Maharashtra for converting into powder. Transporting the milk alone entailed a cost of Rs 2/litre, with conversion charges adding another Re 1. On top of it, the Bangalore and Kolkata dairies weren't generating much business,' recalls Chandramogan.

In May 2004, the company took stock. It was decided to first revise the price of milk sold by the Belgaum dairy upwards by Rs 2 per litre and concentrate on increasing penetration in smaller, but nearby markets such as Hubli-Dharwad, Bagalkot, Raichur, Gulbarga and Goa, rather than large but distant Pune. This was a tried-and-tested Hatsun formula. By September, the lease contract with the Balan dairy at Bangalore had been terminated. The Kolkata milk operations were also wound up towards July 2005, and the 'Delight' brand sold back to its original owner for Rs 9 lakh, Rs 18 lakh less than the value at which it had been bought.

All this did not seem to perturb Chandramogan overly, though. 'During this period, two of our senior general managers resigned, claiming that the company was sinking and leaving us in the lurch. But Chandramogan was calm and confident that things would turn around once the new powder and concentrated milk plants were ready,' recounts K.S. Thanarajan, the then joint managing director.

Chandramogan's optimism was based on two facts. First, September–January was the 'flush' season, when production by cows tended to go up roughly 25 per cent. The company could choose not to take the extra milk supplied by farmers at this time, especially when it had only a single functional ten tonnes-per-day powder plant. But for Chandramogan, that amounted to short-termism. It linked up to the second point: once the new powder and concentrated milk facilities were up and running by the year-end, there wouldn't be any need to undertake conversion in Maharashtra, leading straightaway to savings of Rs 3/litre. That, on 1.25 LLPD, worked out to over Rs 1.1 crore per month.

'Further, we were entering the 2005 summer season, when both ice cream sales would pick up, and milk procurement would slow down down in the natural course. I wasn't too worried, therefore, about losses in one quarter. On the contrary, this was the time to retain farmers' loyalty and ensure that our newly-commissioned plants got enough milk to run to full capacity,' he points out. Chandramogan's strategic thinking— forgoing short-term profits, making investments that would pay in the long term, and effecting cost savings wherever possible— was proved right. HAP's profits after tax fell from Rs 5.39 crore in 2003–04 to Rs 73.51 lakh in 2004–05. The benefits from the new investments were, however, seen in the following fiscal, when not only did net sales go up by a fifth to Rs 540.34 crore, but profits after tax also recovered to Rs 4.25 crore.

Marketing overhaul

The first half of the decade also witnessed a significant restructuring of the company's marketing network. As mentioned previously, HAP had, by 2000–01, established a chain of about seventy clearing & forwarding agents and 2,500 retailers for 'Arokya' milk alone. The agents or super stockists were the ones whom the company billed against the supply of material. They, in turn, collected payments mostly in cash from the retailers, who exclusively sold 'Arokya' milk. When Ajith Dairy was acquired, the first thing HAP did was to stop all bulk loose milk sales in fibre reinforced plastic/stainless steel tankers. Initially, 'Komatha' pouch toned milk was marketed through Ajith Dairy's distributors. But since they were pushing other brands as well, the company appointed independent dealers for 'Komatha'. The retailers and provision stores to whom they supplied, however, sold not only 'Komatha,' but also 'Aavin' and other milk brands.

'In effect, we were running two marketing networks. The first comprised the super stockists and Arokya exclusive outlets, who were already selling our standardized 4.5 per cent fat milk. The second was the Komatha distributors-provision stores chain. The first lot weren't interested in Komatha milk, and we let them be. The provision shop owners were willing to sell, but only if we provided the margins and incentives available on other brands,' says Chandramogan's son Sathyan, who had just taken over as executive director (operations).

'Komatha' was launched for the mass-market toned milk segment through the provision store routes across Tamil Nadu from 2001 onwards. At its peak, 'Komatha' sales hit nearly one LLPD, but this was basically on the back of monthly 'budget cards' and other consumer promotion schemes. It was difficult to sustain when the product (toned milk with 3 per cent fat) had no real USP and was pitted against an established brand like 'Aavin'. Moreover, while the Arokya exclusive outlets maintained milk chillers, guaranteeing product shelf-life wasn't easy with 'Komatha'. Even if the distributor had the cold chain to prevent spoilage, enforcing it on provision store owners was a different ball game. By the end of 2005, HAP had stopped all sales of 'Komatha' milk. Whatever little toned milk it marketed now was under the 'Hatsun' brand.

The decision to bring back the focus on 'Arokya' was also reinforced by Chandramogan's interactions with the American marketing guru Al Ries, who, along with Jack Trout, had propounded the idea of 'brand positioning'. Chandramogan had read their famous 1981 work *Positioning: The Battle for Your Mind*. Sometime in September 2003, he sent two emails to Ries, seeking his brand consultancy services. Ries did not respond and replied only to a third email, in which Chandramogan had mentioned that he was planning a visit to the US and wouldn't mind flying down to Atlanta to meet him. Ries not only granted an appointment, but after being convinced of Chandramogan's seriousness, accepted an invitation to come over to Chennai.

'He wanted $30,000 for a one-day session plus business class air tickets and accommodation, including for his daughter Laura. I offered to pay $60,000 for three days, apart from taking care of their flight and hotel expenses,' confides Chandramogan, who also got two other Chennai-based companies, Reynolds Pens India and

Shriram Chits, to share the $60,000 tab for individual one-day sessions with Al Ries.

Al and Laura Ries arrived in December 2003. 'It was he who told us to sell Arokya not as standardized milk but as milk with 4.5 per cent fat. According to him, positioning was all about occupying the consumer's mind space and distinguishing one's product from that of the competitors. So, instead of using the term standardized milk, it was the 4.5 per cent number that needed highlighting in order to position Arokya properly. Coming from a western marketing professional, it gave us the confidence that the strategy of pushing Arokya over Komatha wasn't misplaced,' reveals Chandramogan.

In early 2004, HAP unveiled an ad campaign titled '*Arjun Amma Yaaru?* (Who is Arjun's Mom)'. It featured a boy by the name of Arjun who excelled both in studies and games. The fifteen-second daily promotional teasers simply asked who this bright lad's mother was. The two-week-long series ended with introducing the mother. She was the one who bought 'Arokya' milk daily and made sure that her son drank this '*naalarai paal* (4.5 milk)'. 'Arokya' milk, in other words, got identified with '*naalarai paal*' or the 4.5 per cent number, as per Al Ries' advice. The latter continued to provide consultancy services to Chandramogan, which was gratis and over telephone calls made from Chennai!

The 'Komatha' experiment wasn't a waste nevertheless. In August 2001, HAP started making around 150 kg per day of 'Dairy Choice' cup-curd from the Ramalingapuram plant, which had been producing *khoa* that wasn't doing well. In 2003, it was decided to re-launch curd in both cups and packets under the 'Komatha' brand, while being pushed through its marketing channel. By 2005-end, even this product got rebranded as 'Hatsun' curd. But unlike toned milk, it turned out to be a success and went on to be the company's second-biggest revenue source—after 'Arokya' milk and on par with 'Arun' ice cream! At that point in time, no

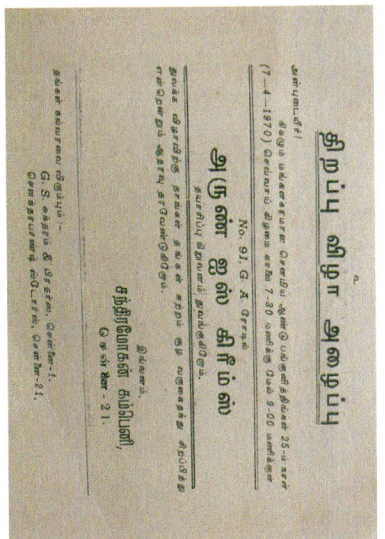
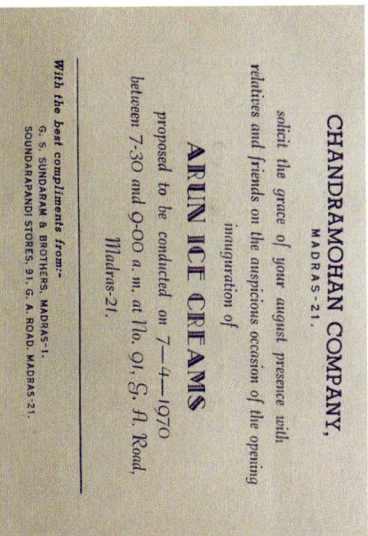

Invitations for the opening of the Arun ice cream factory on 7 April 1970, the first one in Tamil and the second in English.

R.G. Chandramogan (sitting first from left) with his production managers Shankaran Kutty (centre) and Pavithran (right), employees and vendors at the Arun ice cream factory in 1977.

Chandramogan (third from right) with employees at the
Arun ice cream factory premises.

Arun ice cream vendor Duraipandian.

Chandramogan standing in front of his old 650 sq ft rented premise
at Royapuram that is still known as 'Arun ice cream factory'.

Chandramogan with pushcart vendor and tricycle
operator S.M Prakash at Arun ice cream's first
major factory in North Chennai's Tollgate.

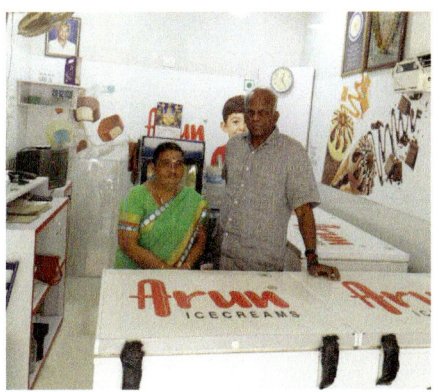

Chandramogan with Dhanalakshmi, owner of
the first Arun ice cream 'sit-and-eat' parlour at
Mannarswamy Koil Street in Royapuram.

Actor Ramya Krishnan promoting Arun ice cream
in 1986, when she was just sixteen years old.

Fast bowler Javagal Srinath giving away the awards at an Arun ice cream 'slow two-wheeler race' show in January 1990, when he wasn't an international-level cricketer yet.

Chandramogan with 'brand positioning' marketing gurus Al and Laura Ries.

Actor Radhikaa endorsing Arokya milk in 2000.

A Tamil ad campaign in 2004 promoting Arokya as 'Naalarai Paal' (4.5% fat milk). It talks about the product helping children develop "lightning speed minds".
The actor Radhikaa endorsing Arokya milk ad is dated 2000.

K.S. Thanarajan (middle) and C. Sathyan (left) with Chandramogan.

Farmers bringing their cows to a free veterinary camp organised by Hatsun Agro Product.

A farmer harvesting Co-3 fodder grass using brush-cutter.

A farmer feeding Co-3 grass to her animals.

The Palacode dairy of Hatsun Agro.

Dr John Henry Niezen, ex-head of Hatsun's animal husbandry team.

Farmers outside a Hatsun Milk Bank.

The milk sample of a farmer being offered for testing of fat and
SNF . . .

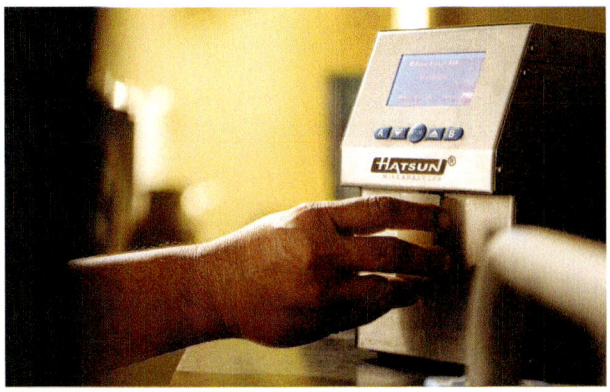

. . . Getting tested.

Chandramogan with farmers at a village in Maharashtra's Solapur district.

Chandramogan with project engineers at the site of Hatsun's new dairy at Shirashi in Maharashtra.

An 'Arokya' milk banner being put over the signboard of a Hatsun Daily-Long Life store during the Covid lockdown period, when ice cream sales took a hit.

Consumers keeping social distancing outside a Hatsun Daily outlet during the lockdown.

organized dairy in the South was seriously into the marketing of curd.

'A couple of private players from Andhra Pradesh, including Heritage, had started selling the product, but we were the first to recognize its true potential. The market we identified was young married working women who had no time to set curd at home from milk. Further, the curd wouldn't form properly during the winter or rainy season. For us, it was an opportunity to target this consumer segment by offering ready-made curd,' observes Chandramogan.

In 2005, another new marketing experiment was unveiled. In June that year, HAP opened a 'home delivery centre' at Vannanthurai in Chennai's Besant Nagar neighbourhood. Consumers could come to the centre and pay an advance amount for up to two months, against which they would get 'Arokya' and 'Komatha' milk (plus curd) directly delivered to their homes. Since the advance payment guaranteed a minimum sale order, the buyer was also eligible for a discount relative to the standard maximum retail price. The experiment didn't click, but Sathyan, whose brainchild it was, decided to convert the home delivery centre into a Hatsun Distribution Centre or HDC. The HDC would no longer deliver milk and curd to homes and, instead, supply only to provision stores and tea shops/restaurants in the area. They would, in turn, reach out to the end-consumer. In the Besant Nagar locality alone, the HDC covered a universe of around 200 retailers, 50 tea shops/restaurants and 7,000 households.

'The 2,500-odd Arokya exclusive retailers we were having in 2001 had crossed 7,000 at the start of 2005. But many of them were now selling only 50–60 litres per day, which wasn't viable enough for us to enforce exclusivity. We saw the HDC model as a means to address this issue,' states Sathyan. Every HDC, housed in a 250–350 square feet space for which the company paid the rent (initially, electricity as well), would be equipped with two chillers of 400 litres each to store the products at about 3 degrees Celsius. It would open at 4.45 a.m. and run till 11.00 p.m. The HDC franchisee was to also have a polyurethane foam insulation ice box, in which the milk pouches or packed curd could be kept for taking on a bike and supplying to retailers. Further, he would supply only to provision stores having refrigeration facilities.

There were three HDCs to start with, all in Chennai: the one at Besant Nagar, a second near the Saligramam bus terminus and the third at Thana Street in Purasawalkam. By 2005-end, there were a total of fourteen. Those numbers proliferated to 260 in 2006, 539 in 2007, 951 in 2008, 1,292 in 2009 and 1,343 in 2010. The HDC franchisees included the erstwhile 'Arokya' exclusive retailers (who could now generate more volumes by becoming suppliers to retailers) and the 'Komatha' dealers (who were distributing both 'Arokya' milk and 'Hatsun' curd, which was registering good growth). An average HDC during this period did daily milk and curd volumes of 250 litres, which, in later years, rose to 900–1,000 litres.

Sathyan reckons that in 2005, 60 per cent of HAP's sales were through Arokya exclusive outlets. By early-2009, over 75 per cent was via the HDCs, who the company was directly billing. In the process, the super-stockists, whose numbers had reached 130 at the start of 2005, were slowly rendered redundant. They were essentially taking milk delivery from HAP's plants in 9,000–12,000 litre refrigerated trucks and re-distributing this to Arokya exclusive retailers in small covered vehicles. But with the HDCs becoming viable and the company directly dealing with them, the super-stockists were eliminated by 2009-end.

The other significant development of this period was 'Arun' ice cream being launched in Seychelles and Brunei, which both had an expatriate Tamil population of 6,000–7,000 each. The lead, not surprisingly, came from the diaspora businessmen themselves. In Seychelles, it was Ramakrishnan Pillay, a fast-moving consumer goods and durables dealer, who approached Chandramogan. The Brunei party was V. Jayakumar, owner of the JPRI Group of companies having similar trading operations. In September 2004, HAP exported its first ice cream consignment to Seychelles. Two months later, another such shipment in 20-foot refrigerated containers to Brunei followed. Within no time, 'Arun' ice cream had grabbed a 70 per cent share of the market in Seychelles and emerged as one of the top four brands in Brunei.

Connecting with farmers

Consolidation of front-end marketing was one part. No less important was bringing about efficiencies at the backend raw material supply front. Hatsun, as we have already seen, was committed to procuring milk directly from farmers. For Chandramogan, it was a sound business strategy more than social service. Besides eliminating intermediaries, direct procurement ensured stable milk supplies throughout the year. That required investing in farmer loyalty, making it worthwhile for them to deliver even in the lean months when others, including small-time operators, would bid up prices.

Between 1999–2000 and 2005–06, HAP's average milk procurement had soared from 1.48 LLPD to 9.75 LLPD, which included 8.60 LLPD from Tamil Nadu and the balance 1.15 LLPD from Karnataka. But in 2005–06, the share of direct milk purchases from farmers in the total procurement was just over 37 per cent, with bulk vendors supplying the rest. This, despite the company's farmer-supplier base (those pouring on a regular basis) expanding to 49,672, from 15,620 at the start of the decade. The company had further quadrupled its veterinary care staff, comprising doctors and artificial insemination workers, to almost 100. The main reason for the high bulk vendor dependence—practically 100 per cent in Thimmasamudram and Belgaum, while 60 per cent for

Karumapuram—was the ever-increasing requirement of milk that couldn't be fully met through direct procurement.

But Chandramogan knew this was unsustainable; there was no alternative to cutting out middlemen in the long run. The challenge here was to get individual farmers to supply more milk, reducing the company's operational and logistics costs. Chandramogan, moreover, did not want to stop there: 'My goal was to work with the farmer, so as to reduce his production cost of milk itself'.

Hatsun, right from end-1995, had started engaging veterinarians on its various milk routes, each covering fifteen to twenty collection centres. From mid-1997, it offered artificial insemination service support and purchased groundnut-cake feed in bulk to supply farmers on a no-profit basis. 'Besides, we conducted animal camps, where farmers brought their cows to our veterinary doctors. In 1999, we had a camp at Navakkurichi in Attur *taluka* of Salem district to treat over 3,500 animals. An even bigger one was held in 2002 at Manjini in the same *taluka*. In addition, we organized free eye-care camps and sponsored cataract operations for farmers in association with the Aravind Eye Hospital, Madurai. The first one was way back in 1995 at Pungavadi, again near Attur. The idea was to build relations with farmers and the larger village community,' informs Chandramogan.

In 1997, HAP set up a Hatsun Training & Research Centre along with a ten-animal dairy farm, next to the Karumapuram plant. 'It was meant to be a model farm, where we would give a practical demonstration of how milk yields can go up and production costs be reduced using the latest feeding and animal management practices. We deputed a veterinarian (one Dr M. Murugesan) and six others to take care of the animals. But it was a total failure. Our ten cows were initially producing some 163 litres per day, which we managed to bring down to 64 litres or so,' says Chandramogan half in jest. The reason: the overheads were too high. In regular farms, the family members themselves did much of the animal rearing and milking work. Also, the seven men on the company's payroll couldn't match the efficiency, leave alone commitment and personal attention to the cows that a family farm could bring. There was no way that production costs could come down.

In 2000, while on a tour to the US, Chandramogan was taken to a dairy farm on the outskirts of Chicago towards North Manchester by Kirtikant Parshotamdas Shah. Shah was a non-resident Indian who had taken a 5 per cent stake in HAP and been appointed as a director. The farm belonged to a Jewish couple, Theresa and Martin. After spending a day watching them manage their 300 animals at the farm, Chandramogan invited the two over to India. They came after two months and stayed at the company's guest house in Salem.

'I took them to our dairy farm. The first thing that Martin did was to take the fresh dung passed by one of the cows with his bare hands. It naturally shocked everybody, including our veterinary doctor, to see a white man do that so comfortably. He was gauging whether the animal's digestion was proper. That could be done by just feeling the heat of the dung and checking out the extent of undigested fibre. I liked their down-to-earth approach, but their feeding and farming systems were different at the end of the day. They had 300 cows and 300 acres of land to grow their own fodder, which couldn't be replicated here,' notes Chandramogan, who around this time also visited the Marmum Dairy Farm in Dubai. 'Its manager was an Indian dairy professional by the name of Dr Arjun Subramanian. The farm had only fourteen people looking after 1,000-plus animals, as opposed to our seven men for ten cows. But I was convinced that their levels of automation, entailing huge capital costs, wouldn't work in India. We needed a model, where the number of animals was optimal for a family-run farm, and milk yields could rise with improved feed management and selective mechanization,' he adds.

The big breakthrough had to wait till about 2004. In May that year, John Perrin, a New Zealand-based dairy farm consultant, visited Salem. Chandramogan was aware of New Zealand being the world's most economical milk producer and the fact that there were probably more lessons to be learnt from that country than the US or Europe. Perrin had responded to an ad that Chandramogan had placed in a New Zealand daily for a farm management expert. Before arriving in India—he spent a week seeing farms in and around Salem—Perrin had also met Sathyan, who happened to go to New Zealand.

It was from Perrin that Chandramogan first heard of the term 'crude protein (CP)'. Simply put, an adult cow in India weighing about 450 kg required roughly 750 grams of CP daily just for its essential body maintenance and mobility. Further, it needed another 100 grams for every litre of milk production. The total CP demand for a cow yielding 15 litres daily, thus, came to 2,250 grams. The first and foremost thing was to deliver an animal's CP requirement in the cheapest and most effective way to reduce milk production cost. That could be done by farmers growing high-yielding protein-rich green fodder themselves and reducing purchases of expensive compound cattle feed. In New Zealand, the animals were primarily fed on ryegrass and white clover mix and given concentrates only when in milk.

Perrin felt that the above formula could be adopted in India. He suggested that HAP engage a dairy herd development-cum-fodder specialist for the purpose. The person recommended by him, Shane Whittaker, joined in November 2004. After having provided consultancy to dairy farmers across New Zealand, Europe and the US, he was working in London. Whittaker interacted with scientists at the Tamil Nadu Agricultural University's (TNAU) Department of Forage Crops in Coimbatore, who had bred 'Co-3,' a hybrid cross between indigenous fodder *bajra* (pearl millet) and

Napier grass native to Africa. Farmers could cultivate this hybrid that yielded 120–130 tonnes of fodder annually per acre over seven or eight harvests every forty to forty-five days. Co-3 had 20 per cent 'dry matter' (from which energy is derived), with CP content at 10 per cent of the latter.

Farmers usually fed their cattle hardly 15 kg of fodder daily. Whittaker's team at Hatsun, along with the TNAU scientists, showed they could be fed 40 kg of Co-3 fodder, which more than met the base 750-gram CP requirement. The dry cows were not producing milk and, therefore, didn't need to be given any concentrates. The ones producing could be fed 40 kg of Co-3 plus another 7 kg of Desmanthus (hedge lucerne) fodder, having twice the former's CP content. Together, these would supply about 9.4 kg of dry matter and 1,080 grams of CP, nearly half of a cow's corresponding requirement of 18 kg and 2,250 grams to produce 15 litres of milk.

'We demonstrated that by reducing reliance on groundnut cake or factory-made concentrates, the feed cost per litre of milk can be brought down substantially. It could further come down if the Co-3 fodder yield was raised to 150 tonnes per acre (from the normal 120–130 tonnes average) and farmers used brush-cutters (to save harvesting labour) along with rain-guns (to halve water consumption). We estimated that these measures halved the overall feed cost to below Rs 5 per litre. Even adding other costs, a farmer could earn a margin of Rs 3.5–4 from supplying milk at Rs 10,' states Chandramogan.

The next step was to take this model to the farmer's field. In late-2006, HAP launched a White Gold Project, targeting the creation of 4,000 'pure' dairy farms over five years. These were to involve individual farmers owning 5–6 acres, who dedicated their entire land to cultivate high-quality fodder and rear milch animals. On their five acres, they would grow Co-3 fodder on roughly 3.5 acres, Desmanthus on one acre and multi-cut sorghum on half-an-acre. Around 0.1 acres was required also to house stalls and milking parlour space for forty cows, at 90 square feet per animal.

'Dairying was always viewed in India as a subsidiary activity to regular crop agriculture. We wanted to introduce a new concept of farmers taking up dairying as a full-time business. They would grow only fodder on their land and add value to the crop by converting it into milk using cows. Under our conditions, the optimal herd size was thirty to forty animals, which also allowed for partial mechanization via brush-cutters, fodder-choppers, rain-guns and milking machines. It was possible for a farmer supplying 300 litres per day (not all cows were in-milk at a time) at Rs 3–3.5/litre margin to earn a monthly income of Rs 27,000–31,500, comparable to the salary of a mid-level government employee,' sums up Chandramogan.

From HAP's standpoint, the major gain from this model was the savings in collection and transport cost. The 4,000 'pure' dairy farmers could potentially supply 12 LLPD of milk, more than the company's average procurement of 10.72 LLPD in 2006–07. The latter was, moreover, from 73,326 farmers, excluding those supplying through bulk vendors. Collecting milk from so many scattered farms was both costly and a logistical challenge. That could be considerably reduced through the White Gold Project, under which HAP even arranged loans for farmers from institutions such as State Bank of India, ICICI Bank, City Union Bank and Indian Bank. The loans would be repaid by deducting from the milk payments against assured purchase by the company. The investment requirement for a 30-cow farm came to about Rs 9 lakh, which included Rs 6 lakh on the animals and the rest towards shed and equipment.

One indicator of HAP's backend extension work paying off was its average milk procurement reaching 13.97 LLPD by 2010–11. The share of direct purchases in that—there were 116,989 regular pourers by now—was over 59 per cent, while close to 70 per cent in Tamil Nadu. The foundations were truly laid for the complete elimination of bulk vendors over the next four to five years. Critical to it was establishing farmer trust through actions beyond plain symbolism. There was one occasion, on 10 June 2007, when the company, faced with a milk glut its existing plants just couldn't handle, had to tell farmers not to supply in the evening shift. Yet, farmers were paid full money for the milk that was not collected—a sum of Rs 40.21 lakh—based on the quantities they had delivered a day earlier! A few years later, two similar 'milk holidays'—on 11 and 24 June, 2015—led to a total monetary outgo of Rs 1.55 crore.

Big-ticket dairies

The second half of the 2000s saw HAP commissioning four new dairies. The first one was at Honnali in Karnataka's Davanagere district, where it already operated a chilling centre. The plant, which came up in April 2007 at a cost of Rs 3.6 crore, had the capacity to process one LLPD of liquid milk for sale in pouches. Being in central Karnataka, it could feed markets in the state's southern parts—Shimoga, Chitradurga, Udupi, Mangalore, Chikmagalur, Tumkur and even Bangalore—that the Belgaum dairy wasn't able to easily do.

The second plant, also a pouch milk facility with 2 LLPD capacity costing Rs 5.45 crore and set up around the same time, was at Thiruvalavayanallur in Madurai district's Vadipatti *taluka*. This area, too, had an existing packing station for liquid milk being supplied loose through tankers from the Karumapuram dairy. The new stand-alone dairy could now better service southern Tamil Nadu markets such as Madurai, Theni, Dindigul, Virudhunagar, Sivakasi, Rajapalayam, Devakottai, Karaikudi, Tirunelveli, Tenkasi and Thoothukudi.

The third dairy, commissioned in April 2009 at a cost of Rs 6.23 crore, was at Thalaivasal, about 65 km from the

Karumapuram facility. Thalaivasal was a major milk belt: HAP was procuring 80,000–90,000 litres daily from just this area and even had a chilling centre there. Besides, it was nearer to markets towards the east coast, mainly Villupuram, Pondicherry, Cuddalore, Nagapattinam, Mayiladuthurai, Thanjavur, Kumbakonam and Trichy. So, the milk being taken earlier to Karumapuram could henceforth be processed at the 2 LLPD Thalaivasal plant.

But the biggest of the four new plants was at Kolasanahalli in Palacode *taluka* of north-west Tamil Nadu's Dharmapuri district. Like in Thalaivasal, the company previously ran a chilling centre that was about 3 km away at a place called Vellichandai. Entailing an investment of Rs 139.26 crore, the Kolasanahalli facility had a 60 tonnes-per-day skimmed milk powder (SMP) and 30 tonnes-per-day anhydrous milk fat (AMF) production capacity, equivalent to handling 7.2 LLPD of milk, plus another 1.3 LLPD for pouch milk sales. The greenfield unit commissioned in October 2009 was erected on a turnkey basis by Alfa Laval. The company also appointed two dairy professionals from New Zealand—Jonathan Williams and his wife Tania Huia Williams—to oversee production operations and quality control.

Building what was south India's largest milk processing plant was significantly motivated by the boom in global dairy trade from the mid-2000s. HAP's own export revenues, largely from SMP, rose from a mere Rs 6.16 crore in 2004–05 to Rs 77.45 crore in 2005–06, and further to Rs 112.80 crore in 2007–08 and Rs 190.22 crore in 2008–09. This came on the back of international SMP prices (New Zealand quotes) soaring from an average $ 1,430 per tonne in 2002–03 to $ 2,110 in 2004–05 and $ 4,560 by 2007–08. The company sought to cash in on the boom by offering high-quality dairy ingredients, including SMP and AMF, at competitive prices in south-east Asia, west Asia and Africa, taking advantage of India's geographical proximity to these markets. It also incorporated a 100 per cent wholly-owned subsidiary—Hatsun

Ingredients FZE—at Ras Al Khaimah in the United Arab Emirates, which started operations in April 2009.

'The idea behind establishing such a massive facility was twofold. First, we needed a plant that could handle the extra 25–30 per cent milk during the flush season from August-end to January. Dharmapuri and adjoining Krishnagiri were once upon a time leftwing Naxalite-infested districts, which we had practically on our own developed into a milk belt. The uneven terrain made regular crop agriculture difficult in the area, but we knew that farmers there could be encouraged to take up dairying. Our Vellichandai chilling centre, in fact, came up as early as 2001. Palacode also wasn't very far from major milk sheds in neighbouring states, such as Kolar in Karnataka and Chittoor in Andhra Pradesh. All this milk could be processed in the new dairy. Secondly, we were bullish on exports and envisaged no problems in disposing of the SMP and AMP, particularly with the premium quality of product from our state-of-the-art plant,' observes Chandramogan.

All those calculations came to nought, however, when international SMP prices crashed to $ 1,750 per tonne by February 2009, following the global financial crisis. The Palacode dairy, funded partly through a Rs 60-crore term loan from South Indian Bank, was still under construction then. Even after commissioning in October 2009, it had teething problems and became fully functional only from May 2010. By this time, HAP's debt-equity ratio had deteriorated further. As of 31 March 2010, its total secured and unsecured loans of Rs 313.74 crore were nearly six times the company's share capital and reserves of Rs 53.52 crore— worse than the four times at the end of 2004–05!

'We never faced a worse crisis, before or after. It was again a result of animal spirits and too much expansion within a short period,' confesses Chandramogan. And the problem this time extended to working capital. That had never been an issue even during the previous financial crisis five years ago, as the company obtained raw material (milk) on credit from farmers. There were hardly any trade receivables on its products (branded liquid milk and ice cream) sold on a cash-and-carry basis. But Hatsun was now also in the commodity business of SMP and AMF, which entailed working capital getting stuck in the event of stocks piling up. In 2008–09, exports contributed Rs 190.22 crore or 18.78 per cent of its sales of Rs 1,013.05 crore—which crossed the Rs 1,000-crore mark for the first time. But in the following year, as global prices crashed, export revenues plunged to Rs 46.51 crore, and the company had to liquidate stocks at a loss.

Back to basics

'The one big lesson we learnt was to refocus on branded consumer-facing products, which was our real strength, and move away from the highly volatile commodity business. There was too much of risk here, not only from global prices but also the Union government's unpredictable policies of suddenly withdrawing incentives or even banning exports of milk powder, such as that during February-September 2007,' remarks Chandramogan. The Ras Al Khaimah subsidary was wound up with effect from November 2009.

In 2009–10, HAP's profits after tax fell to Rs 2.69 crore, from Rs 11.97 crore and Rs 17.33 crore for the preceding two fiscals. By the middle of 2009, the company had accumulated roughly Rs 25 crore worth of unsold stocks of SMP from its Karumapuram and Thimmasamudram plants. With no bank willing to provide working capital against these stocks, HAP, in July 2009, was forced to issue unsecured compulsorily convertible debentures bearing a 6 per cent coupon rate (interest) for a total value of Rs 25 crore. A significant part of it—Rs 11 crore—was subscribed by Kirtikant Shah's family. The rest was allotted to Integrated Registry Services (a Chennai-based financial services company), V.V.V. & Sons Edible Oils (the owners of 'Idhayam' sesame oil brand),

M. Chellayan (whose family had only two years earlier sold Nilgiri
Dairy Farm to the UK private equity investor Actis) and a few
other high net worth individuals. 'These investors bailed us out.
They helped shore up our equity, which was necessary to obtain
bank finance. Banks were obviously uncomfortable lending to a
company with such a high debt-equity ratio,' adds Chandramogan.

In 2009–10, the last financial year of the decade, Hatsun wasn't
only South India's but also the country's largest private-sector
dairy concern. It had an installed milk handling capacity of about
27 LLPD spread over eight locations: Karumapuram (6 LLPD),
Thimmasamudram (4.7 LLPD), Belgaum (1.5 LLPD), Honnali
(1.5 LLPD), Vadipatti (2 LLPD), Thalaivasal (2 LLPD), Palacode
(8.5 LLPD) and Nallur (ice cream plant). Three of these dairies
could produce 95 tonnes per day of powder (Palacode 60 tonnes,
Karumapuram 25 tonnes and Thimmasamudram 10 tonnes). In
2009–10, the Nallur ice cream factory's capacity, too, had been
expanded to 50,000 litres per day. Out of the company's net sales
of Rs 1,140.60 crore that year, Rs 762.68 crore came from liquid
milk (9.48 LLPD), Rs 145.47 crore from milk powder (11,939
tonnes) and Rs 75.17 crore from ice cream (82.67 lakh litres).

For Hatsun and Chandramogan, the story of the 1970s and
1980s had been about ice cream, while the following two decades
was that of becoming an integrated dairy enterprise and emerging
as India's leading private player in the sector. But it was also a
journey of trial and error—even outright mistakes, some near-
fatal. The important thing was learning from them, retracting
where necessary, and keeping the entrepreneurial spirit alive by
doing things not many would.

One such experiment towards the decade-end that failed, but
yielded useful lessons for the future was 'Sikkanam,' a rural retail
venture. At the time of its launch, in April 2008, HAP had nearly
5,000 milk collection centres. Each centre was housed in a 125–
150 square feet space, with only 20–30 square feet of it actually

being used for receiving, testing, weighing and keeping the milk bought from farmers. There was, thus, an average unutilized area of 100–120 square feet, adding up to nearly 6 lakh square feet across all collection centres.

'This spare space, we thought, could be used to stock and sell groceries and other household items to the same farmers who were pouring milk at our centres. The very vehicles collecting milk could also deliver the products that were to be sold. The centres operated, depending on location, from around 6.30 to 8.30 a.m. and 5.30 to 7.30 p.m. We were anyway paying for their rent and electricity, whereas the vehicles ran empty one way. Rural retail was simply a means for using our space and logistics infrastructure more effectively, apart from providing extra income for the centre operators. They were all largely local village boys who only earned commission from milk procurement,' informs Chandramogan.

'Sikkanam' (Tamil for budget) was conceived as a network of no-frills rural stores. Fundamentally, it was a sound concept. Within two years, as many as 980 outlets had come up, retailing up to 120 SKUs (stock-keeping units). These included daily provisions (rice, *dal*, sugar and edible oils), toiletries (soap, toothbrush and toothpaste) and durables such as *lungis*, bed sheets, stainless steel vessels, electric rice cookers, tiffin boxes, casseroles, umbrellas and torch lights. The items were procured in bulk and delivered to the Sikkanam stores from the erstwhile Vellichandai chilling centre, which now served as a warehousing hub. The company made sure no product was sold on credit, though the practically zero extra logistics costs allowed them to be even supplied at below maximum retail prices.

Yet, Sikkanam wasn't the success that it should have been. The flaw lay in the difference between what was being procured from the centres and the stuff getting retailed. The former was a single product—milk—while the latter were multiple SKUs. That apart, milk being perishable left a very narrow time window for any vehicle to cover some fourteen centres in a single route. If the same vehicle collecting milk also had to offload multiple items that were to be separately accounted for, it further complicated the task. 'It's not that the margins were low or we were losing money in retail, but the nature of the two businesses was like chalk and cheese. They required totally different approaches,' sums up Chandramogan.

Drawing lessons from mistakes was, of course, hardwired into Hatsun's DNA. In this case, the big takeaway was to recognize that HAP was ultimately a dairy company and anything it wanted to sell—including to farmers—had to have some connection with milk. That connection was to be found through cattle feed. In the coming decade, the company was to sell compound balanced cattle feed to its dairy producers. This, again, had to be high-quality, branded, and manufactured at its own facility. And being a single large-volume commodity just like milk, there wouldn't be issues with regard to delivery, even while guaranteeing more optimal utilization of collection centre space and logistical resources.

5

A Corporate Social Enterprise

K. Maran Kumar delivers 15 litres of milk on an average daily—8 litres in the morning shift (from 7.00 to 8.30 a.m.) and 7 in the evening (from 6.00 to 7.30 p.m.)—to HAP's collection centre at Jeenur village in Krishnagiri district and *taluka*. The moment he brings the milk, the person at the Hatsun Milk Bank (HMB), as the centre is called, draws a 90-ml sample and puts it in an automatic stirrer for ten seconds to remove air bubbles. The testing-ready sample is next placed on an Ekomilk Ultra Pro analyser, even as Kumar's producer code gets entered on a keyboard. In some forty seconds, the ultrasonic analyser shows his milk to have 5.1 per cent fat and 8.4 per cent SNF (solids-not-fat) content. After testing, Kumar's entire consignment is taken to a connected electronic weighing scale, and the keyboard punched again. The display screen in the Ekomilk analyser now indicates the total quantity poured (8.04 litres), the rate corresponding to the fat-SNF content in the sample (Rs 31.6/litre) and the payment due (Rs 254.06), besides the date and time of supply. All this happens before Kumar, who also gets an SMS alert giving the same details.

The beauty of the system is its transparency. Not only is the farmer paid for quality—the Rs/litre rates, based on a two-way price chart against different fat/SNF percentage combinations, are directly fed into the analyser—but he gets to 'see' everything. Moreover, the Ekomilk analyser, unlike the traditional Gerber-lactometer method of estimating fat/SNF content that uses chemicals (sulphuric acid and amyl alcohol) and requires a minimum batch of testing samples, provides instant results. Kumar doesn't have to wait till twenty-three or twenty-four others deliver their samples. With the analyser, there also isn't scope for the centre-in-charge to play favourites, by swapping one farmer's sample with another's. Every transaction is recorded: the moment the keyboard is punched, the data entered in the Ekomilk machine gets transferred through GPRS (general packet radio service) mobile communications to HAP's remote central cloud server. Payment is directly made by the company, with the HMB person having no role there either. Kumar's money is credited straight into his Bank of India account at its Krishnagiri branch. Such direct transfer, made against his producer code and bank account number, takes place once every ten days.

Along with it, Kumar gets a consolidated statement of the shift-wise milk supply details for all the ten days. The cumulative payment for the first ten days' supplies happens on the twelfth or thirteenth of that month. Similar transfers are done for the quantities poured during the next ten-day cycles, on the twenty-second/twenty-third and second/third.

Maran Kumar is only one out of the 381,456 farmers with unique producer codes, from whom HAP procured 27.26 lakh litres per day (LLPD) of milk on an average during 2019–20. Those numbers, we saw, were only 116,989 and 13.97 LLPD in 2010–11 and 24,659 and 2.85 LLPD in 2000–01. Kumar, and B. Palanisamy of Paiyur village in Krishnagiri district and taluka, are both from Tamil Nadu's most backward region. The two north-eastern districts of Krishnagiri and Dharmapuri, even at the start of the century, were known as Maoist hotbeds. Barely 10 km from HAP's

Kolasanahalli dairy is Padi, the village in Dharmapuri's Palacode *taluka* where the notorious forest brigand Veerappan was gunned down by a special task force of Tamil Nadu police in October 2004. Yet, out of the 27 LLPD-plus of milk that HAP collected during the 2019–20 financial year, over five LLPD came from Dharmapuri and Krishnagiri districts, which no dairy concern, the state-owned Aavin cooperative included, had even tried to develop.

For Kumar and Palanisamy, milk offers a steady and assured source of income, unlike other crops marketed only once or twice a year and prone to price fluctuations. Kumar—his seventy-five-year-old father Kannappan is a retired Naik from the Indian Army—has 3.5 acres of land, on which he grows paddy on two, ragi on 0.5, tomato on 0.5, and Co-4 green fodder on the remaining 0.5 acres. In addition, he has two crossbred Jersey cows—one four-and-a-half years and the other six years eight months old—and two calves aged three months and ten months, respectively. Both cows are over six months pregnant and currently together, yielding only 15 litres of milk daily. This would more than double after they calve within the next three months. By then, one of the two calves will be ready for insemination. Kumar's two acres of paddy yield hardly 40 quintals, worth Rs 64,000 at Rs 1,600/quintal and Rs 30,000 after deducting expenses. He sees more value in the straw than grain, as the former can be fed to the cows that generate regular revenue. Each milking animal is now being given 25 kg of Co-4 fodder and 5 kg of straw daily, both produced from the farm, apart from 2 kg of HAP's 'Santosa' brand compound cattle feed that is bought. 'Milk sales and my father's monthly pension of Rs 38,000 is what keeps our house going,' remarks Kumar.

Palanisamy has ten cows, seven of them in milk, plus five heifers below fourteen months of age and two calves. He supplies about 70 litres daily to HAP, rising to 100 litres during the flush season after September. The thirty-year-old plans to expand his herd size to twenty cows and milk supplies to 200 litres in the next two years. Palanisamy, along with his brother Ravichandran and father Bhimraj, farm just 3 acres. On this, they grow fodder on 2.3 acres—1.5 acres under Co-4, 0.5 acres under sorghum and 0.3 acres under Co-5—and banana on 70 cents. That apart, they have a 0.1-acre pond for rearing tilapia, rohu, mrigal, and catla[1] fish. Palanisamy's 550-odd Elakki banana plants yield 7–9 kg of fruit each. At Rs 40/kg, they gross Rs 1.75 lakh and Rs 1.40–1.45 lakh net of costs. Similarly, his five tonnes annual fish production realize Rs 5 lakh at Rs 100/kg, against expenditures of Rs 2.5 lakh (Rs 2.3 lakh on feed and Rs 20,000 on fingerlings/seed). But it is the sale of milk that provides liquidity, stability and predictability to this enterprising small-grower family.

Game-changers

For Chandramogan, the Ekomilk Ultra Pro analysers were a game-changer. He had first heard of these Bulgarian-make machines being used by Reliance Industries Ltd, which had entered the dairy business in 2007 (only to exit by 2016). 'They had supplied these to their bulk vendors, including in Krishnagiri's Uthangarai taluka. We then decided to install them at our own milk procurement centres,' states Chandramogan. HAP's collection centres, in January 2009, had been rechristened Hatsun Milk Banks or HMBs, to complement the HDCs (Hatsun Distribution Centres) in existence since June 2005. In January 2011, the first HMB equipped with an Ekomilk Ultra Pro analyser system—EKO HMBs, as they came to be known—was opened at Kannipatti in Dharmapuri's Palacode *taluka*.

The benefits to farmers were obvious. They now got payments for milk quality based on fat and SNF content without any room for manipulation by the centre-in-charge, as everything happened in front of everybody. The measurement and recording of the milk solids was instant, and all this data got immediately transmitted to HAP's system through GPRS. Even in places where mobile service providers had no network—about 5 per cent HMBs were in such locations—the data could be captured in USB pen drives and collected by the dairy tankers.

'Earlier, not only farmers, even we were at the HMB man's mercy and had to go by the information he provided—be it on the number of farmers supplying or the total quantity and fat/SNF content of milk they poured. But after the Ekomilk analyzers came, we found the total solids in our milk rising by up to one percentage point in some centres. The average increase was by 0.3–0.4 percentage points. This was partly due to the centre-in-charge no longer being able to add water or show more number of farmers. Also, it was in the farmers' interest now to supply milk with more solids, as they clearly saw the rewards of a transparent measurement and payment system. And we benefited because it meant transporting that much less water to the dairy,' points out Chandramogan.

Between 2009–10 and 2019–20, the number of HMBs went up from 5,197 to 9,101. All of them, in due course, became EKO HMBs. By October 2017, all their buildings—mostly around 150 square feet of rented space—were to have rooftop solar panels of 100 watts per hour capacity each, apart from a battery that could store up to 900 watts of power. These supplied the electricity for running the entire system—including the milk analyser, electronic weighing scale, UPS, stirrer and keyboard—whose requirement was only about 80 watts per hour or 320 watts for two shifts of two hours each. This could be comfortably met from the stored power in the battery, which was charged during the peak sunshine hours (10.30 a.m. to 2.30 p.m.) as well as three to four hours before and after. Electricity from the grid was needed to be drawn only during the 60-odd rainy/cloudy days of the year. With an average investment of Rs 1.25 lakh for the Ekomilk systems and solar panels in every HMB, the total cost of creating this 'transparency-and-trust-creating' infrastructure came to more than Rs 115 crore, although spread over seven to eight years.

As more and more EKO HMBs got established, the company, by June 2015, had completely stopped milk procurement through bulk vendors. That, for Chandramogan, was a major landmark. The story did not end there. Even after the first EKO HMB's opening in January 2011, HAP was making payments for milk in cash. In November that year, it started crediting money into the bank accounts of the centres in charge. The latter, in turn, withdrew cash and made payments as before to farmers; each HMB collected 300 litres daily on an average from thirty to forty farmers.

In November 2014, HAP launched a new initiative of transferring payments directly into farmers' accounts. 'There was initial resistance from the farmers, as they were used to dealing in cash. At that time, dairy cooperatives too, were limiting bank transfers only to the primary village societies (equivalent to HMBs). They further withdrew from their accounts and paid farmers in cash. But we forced our farmers to open bank accounts because arranging cash and transporting it to the already 6,000-plus HMBs was a logistical and security nightmare. No less difficult was to make exact payment to every farmer against varying quantities and fat-SNF content of milk supplied. That, again, gave scope for the centre persons to exercise discretion by holding back or not giving full payment,' notes Chandramogan. By October 2015, just four months after eliminating bulk vendors, HAP had moved to 100 per cent cashless mode to make payments to all its farmers.

The vindication came a little more than a year later. On 8 November 2016, the Narendra Modi government at the Centre announced the scrapping ('demonetization') of all outstanding Rs 500 and Rs 1,000 denomination currency notes. It led to countless businesses facing problems and a spate of payment defaults. However, HAP and its farmers 'slept peacefully,' claims Chandramogan. Between 9 November and 18 November, the company credited payments totalling Rs 64.25 crore to the accounts of 250,964 farmers against milk supplies made during the previous seven to ten days (the payment cycle then varied from place to place before it was decided to adopt a uniform ten-days cut-off).

'Demonetization was a shock, a bolt out of the blue for the economy. But for us, it was business as usual. And we are proud to have gone cashless much before it became part of official policy, post demonetization. Not a single dairy had attempted what we already accomplished by October 2015,' adds Chandramogan. Farmers were also not to regret the move to direct bank transfers. A farmer pouring 10 litres daily at Rs 26–27/litre now got Rs 2,600–2,700 credited to his bank account every ten days. This was substantial money. No less significant, even the bank manager started viewing him as a customer to be wooed rather than as a supplicant or somebody whose loans had to be waived under government pressure.

Deepening engagement

Procuring milk from farmers bypassing all intermediaries and also making direct payments was only the culmination of forging a close working relationship whose seeds were sown much earlier. We have seen how HAP, from around 2005, had collaborated with the Tamil Nadu Agricultural University (TNAU), Coimbatore to promote the cultivation of high-yielding proteinaceous green fodder grasses for reducing reliance on expensive compound cattle feed and oil-meal concentrates. Subsequent to Co-3, the varsity had released two other hybrids, Co-4 and Co-5. These were also crosses of indigenous fodder *bajra* (Pennisetum glaucum) and exotic Napier or elephant grass (Pennisetum purpureum). Their progeny combined the former's easy palatability and digestibility with the latter's high biomass and ruggedness.

The fodder yields from Co-4 and Co-5, at 150–160 tonnes per acre over 7–8 harvests in a year, were more than the 130–140 tonnes of Co-3. The TNAU scientists had, moreover, raised their dry matter content to 22 per cent, as against Co-3's 20 per cent. Crude protein levels, too, were enhanced, from 10 per cent of dry matter in Co-3, to 10.7 per cent for Co-4 and up to 14 per cent for Co-5.

'We did the breeding, but the credit for propagating and taking our hybrids to farmers' fields goes to Hatsun. They were the ones who sourced the stem cuttings (planting material) from us for further multiplication and distribution,' admits Prof C. Babu, head of TNAU's Department of Forage Crops. HAP also, from 2016, started sponsoring the position of a 'Hatsun Chair Assistant Professor' in the department for promoting forage breeding, research and development.

The cultivation cost of Co-5, a perennial grass that could be harvested 75–80 days after planting and with subsequent cuttings at 40–45 day intervals for the next five years, came to roughly Rs 18,000 per acre or Rs 0.12/kg for a yield of 150 tonnes. At 14 per cent on a dry matter content of 20 per cent, the corresponding crude protein cost worked out to just Rs 4.3 per kg. Compound cattle feed and concentrates, by contrast, had a higher dry matter of 90 per cent and with crude protein at 18 per cent of that. But being priced at about Rs 21/kg, the cost of delivering protein via this route was Rs 130 per kg. It was even more, at Rs 222, in the case of paddy straw having only 4 per cent crude protein on 90 per cent dry matter and bought for Rs 8/kg!

'Our focus was to encourage farmers to grow good-quality high-yielding fodder, like in New Zealand and cut down on the purchase of concentrates. Dry animals don't need these at all. Even cows producing 10 litres of milk daily require no cattle feed, if you give 60 kg of Co-5 costing just Rs 7.2 or Rs 0.72 per litre. We have farmers (like B. Palanisamy) who provide 40 kg of green fodder and limit cattle feed use solely for milk production (about 3 kg for 10 litres and 11 kg for 25 litres, which still keeps the overall feeding cost within Rs 6.8–9.5/litre. There are also farmers feeding paddy straw (Maran Kumar, for instance), but gradually taking to Co-4 or Co-5 cultivation,' says Dr John Henry Niezen, ex-head of HAP's animal husbandry team that includes seven territory managers, sixteen veterinary doctors, sixty field supervisors, 375 inseminators and fifty agricultural extension officers. A Canadian dairy herd development specialist based in Australia and New Zealand, he worked with the company from January 2015 to June 2020.

In 2019–20, HAP supplied 35 lakh cuttings of Co-4, Co-5 and 'Pakchong 1 Super Napier,' a hybrid fodder from Thailand, to select farmers. They do the multiplication for reaching out to other farmers within their vicinity (around 11,000 cuttings are planted every acre). The company has, since 2016, also taken up seed production of CoFS-29, a fodder sorghum hybrid developed by TNAU. Although the fodder yield (65 tonnes per acre) and crude protein content (8.5 per cent of dry matter) from it are lower than that of Co-5, CoFS-29 is relatively drought-tolerant. 'We recommend it as a perennial fodder in water-scarce areas. For us, too, it is logistically easier to supply seeds than cuttings,' observes Niezen. HAP, in 2019-20, sold 21 tonnes of CoFS-29 seeds through its field staff and HMBs. The seeds (the sowing rate is 5 kg/acre) are being procured through contract cultivation, which has become a programme in itself.

Meanwhile, the company, in May 2013, had ventured into compound cattle feed manufacture, by taking over a 100 tonnes-per-day plant from SKM Egg Products Exports (India) Ltd. At Noyyal in Karur district, this unit was bought for Rs 8 crore after its erstwhile owner faced repayment issues on a State Bank of India loan. HAP had, since March 1997, been supplying groundnut cake to its farmers. In January 2000, it began sourcing branded cattle feed from different companies and selling these at cost price to its farmers. The next step was to get cattle feed contract manufactured and sell under its own brand—initially 'Hatsun' in January 2002 and, from July 2004, as 'Santosa'. Till the Noyyal plant's acquisition, HAP was making available the feed ingredients to third-party factories. They were paid conversion charges for making and packing the product as per its formula/ specifications.

'We had closed down our Sikkanam rural retail store operations in March 2011. But exploiting the unutilized space in HMBs for selling things to our own farmers was always at the back of our mind. That led to the decision to go for more focussed marketing of balanced cattle feed and ensuring better quality by in-house manufacturing. We don't use any urea that, being highly government-subsidized, is often diverted to replace natural but more expensive protein sources. Our vitaminized feed only has cottonseed oilcake, soy bean meal, de-oiled rice bran, maize and cane molasses. It also contains whey water, a by-product of cheese manufacture that our dairies were earlier discarding. Being very rich in protein, we started using it as a feed ingredient. We strictly adhere to the 20 parts-per-billion limit for aflatoxins (produced by certain fungus moulds growing in soil or grain) in cattle feed, as prescribed by the Bureau of Indian Standards,' emphasizes Chandramogan.

In December 2015, HAP acquired a second feed mill at Melkaraipatti in Palani *taluka* of Dindigul, belonging to an unlisted firm, VKS Farms Pvt. Ltd, for Rs 13.50 crore. It was a 100-tonnes-per-day plant, but the promoter, who was also debt-strapped, had partially completed work on 400 tonnes, besides laying the basic steel structure and storage infrastructure for 800 tonnes. This mill's capacity was subsequently expanded to 900 tonnes per day, while the earlier 100-tonnes unit at Noyyal was converted into an ice cream cold store. Earlier, in July 2015, the company had introduced 'Santosa XL,' a premium feed with 25 per cent crude protein content, as against 18 per cent in the regular bypass pellet formulation. In 2019–20, HAP's cattle feed sales totalled 153,254 tonnes, valued at Rs 354.82 crore.

'Santosa is exclusively sold through HMBs. For us, cattle feed is a means to engage more with our farmers. We simply recover our costs and charge a modest margin on that. The value of feed purchased by farmers is deducted from the payments due against the milk supplied by them. This adjustment is, again, done every ten days and the net amount transferred into their bank accounts,' informs Chandramogan.

In September 2016, HAP took its engagement with farmers a step further—by extending it to their animals. That month, John Niezen's team launched a programme to 'tag' the cows of all farmers supplying milk to the company. Each cow was to have a thermoplastic polyurethane tag attached to its ear, carrying two pieces of information—a twelve-digit unique identification number (just like the 'Aadhaar' UID for Indian citizens) and a corresponding QR barcode. Parallel to this was a Hatsun Animal Information Service (HAIS) database built on Herdman, a platform developed by an Indian software firm Vetware Private Ltd founded by a veterinarian Dr Abdul Samad. Thus, Maran Kumar's both cows have ear tags with distinct animal IDs and QR codes printed on them. The moment a HAP doctor or inseminator scans the QR code of any one of them using a smartphone having the Herdman mobile application, he can access all information relating to it electronically recorded in the HAIS system: name and producer code of her owner, breed type (in this case, Jersey-Gir crossbred), age, current status (pregnant or not), expected date of calving, number and date of last artificial insemination (AI), identity of the bull whose semen was used, etc.

As of 31 March 2020, 5.95 lakh animals had been registered in the HAIS database, out of which 3.72 lakh were giving milk. These would have covered most of the animals from whom HAP was collecting milk, even after excluding the ones that were dry, had stopped calving or gone out of the system. A key objective behind the entire tagging exercise has been to make the company's AI and veterinary interventions more systematic and purposeful.

'HAP's 300-odd inseminators do nearly 4 lakh AIs every year. The average conception rate, at 35–40 per cent, is quite good. But with tagging, we know every animal's pedigree, how many times it has been inseminated and the number of pregnancies resulting from these. We can now ensure the semen used is of a sire different from the one that had inseminated her mother or daughter. Moreover, the company issues SMS alerts to farmers about eighteen days after insemination to check the status of their cows. If they have come to heat, it means no pregnancy and they require fresh insemination. If there's no heat, then pregnancy tests and regular nutrition alerts in the lead up to calving would follow. Also, it's possible to identify infertile, repeat breeder and anoestrus cows. These can, then, be isolated or given treatment. Earlier, all this was a black box, and there was little genetic evaluation backing our AI/veterinary interventions. We merely responded to farmers' requests; it was to inseminate and move on, or treat and move on,' explains Niezen.

HAP charges farmers between Rs 50 and Rs 85 for every AI straw (0.25-ml vials carrying frozen semen) that is used. At a 40 per cent conception rate, it translates into Rs 125–212.5 per pregnancy. The semen, frozen at about minus 190 degrees in liquid nitrogen tanks to ensure sperm viability, is sourced from reputed breeders like the National Dairy Development Board's Sabarmati Ashram Gaushala, BAIF Development Research Foundation, ABS India and Best Sire Genetics & Breeding. The company buys the frozen semen straws in bulk and stores them in four locations for further distribution. According to Niezen, the results from tagging had led to HAP even discontinuing semen purchases from one supplier when the conception rates from its bulls were found to be too low.

'We recover only the material cost, which is electronically deducted from the farmer's bank account. The inseminator's salary, transport and visiting expenses are fully company-subsidized. For us, AI and veterinary services or the provision of fodder and feed aren't money-making activities. They earn us farmer loyalty, inducing them to invest in animal productivity and supply more milk,' avers Chandramogan. He reckons the total cost that HAP incurs on providing AH and veterinary services—not recovered from farmers—at approximately Rs one crore per month. That works out to over 11 paise per litre. Animal tagging is yet another investment that will pay, though not in the short run.

Chandramogan sums up the company's approach: 'The government wants to double farmers' income and guarantee them a minimum 50 per cent return over cost. We believe both are possible. But the right way to do it is not by hiking procurement prices year after year, which will only make Indian agriculture globally uncompetitive. Instead, it should be through bringing down the cost of production. We have demonstrated how farmers can achieve a more than 50 per cent reduction in cow feeding costs by giving them less compound feed/concentrates and growing high-yielding protein-rich fodder hybrids. They can further use brush-cutters to save on harvesting labour and rain-guns for halving water consumption. If the total milk production cost is Rs 10–12 per litre and we are paying Rs 28–30, the farmer's net return is 150–200 per cent! And by procuring and making payments directly, sans any middlemen, the cost savings work out even higher'.

A cool way to chill

Sometime in July 2007, two young men came over to Chandramogan's office at Chennai. Sam White was a Boston-based business development executive. His colleague Sorin Grama was originally from Romania and had just finished his master's in engineering and management from the Massachusetts Institute of Technology (MIT). They were working on a technology to chill milk using a thermal energy battery that was solar-powered. The topic of Grama's thesis happened to be 'A survey of thin-film solar photovoltaic industry & technologies'. He had also won the runner-up prize in MIT's $100K Business Plan Competition for 2007.

What the two techies had in mind was a system that de-coupled the supply of power from chilling. The thermal battery would store electricity from the sun's rays and release this energy to bring down the temperature of a liquid coolant inside it to sub-zero. The battery further had a compressor to pump the coolant—an isopropyl alcohol solution having a freezing point below that of water—through tubes to a separate cylinder-shaped chilling unit. The milk collected from farmers would be poured on the top of the cylinder maintained at around minus three degrees Celsius by the circulating fluid. As the milk went over the cylinder, it also got chilled. This milk could, then, be taken to an insulated storage silo, where it remained chilled.

The basic concept appealed to Chandramogan. At the time he had met the Boston duo, the milk that HAP procured from farmers was being transported by tankers first to chilling centres. By 2007–08, the company had forty-seven such centres, with individual capacities from 20,000 to 50,000 litres. Like in Thalaivasal and Palacode that were to later on house full-fledged dairies, some could even handle 80,000–90,000 litres. A tanker usually collected milk from twelve to fifteen procurement centres/HMBs within a 60–80 km radius of a chilling centre. Once it left a cow's udders, the milk had to ideally be chilled within an hour or hour and a half. After that, the naturally occurring preservatives in the milk (including carbon dioxide) stopped working, and there would be a growth of bacteria that converted the lactose (sugar) into lactic acid. If chilling was delayed beyond four hours, the bacterial count rose to levels that led to souring, curdling and spoilage.

Every tanker, therefore, had to adhere to a very tight schedule of lifting 300-odd litres of milk from each of the twelve to fifteen HMBs and reach the chilling centre in three and a half to four hours. This had to be over by 9.00–9.30 a.m. in the mornings before it got too hot. It also meant that farmers had to start milking their cows very early.

One way to take care of the problem was to chill the milk at the source. Some dairies were already doing this by putting up bulk coolers at their procurement centres. These kept the milk cool at about 4 degrees Celsius till the tanker from the dairy arrived. A major drawback with the bulk coolers, however, was their capacity of 3,000–5,000 litres each. While 3,000 litres was what many individual American or European producers supplied daily—making it viable to have coolers at the farm itself—HAP's procurement centres hardly handled 300 litres, ranging from 275 in the lean to 325 in the flush season. That would have resulted in sub-optimal capacity utilization. Moreover, given the irregular power in rural areas, the bulk coolers required diesel generator backup. It further raised costs, besides causing noise and air pollution.

'I liked their idea of separating the supply of power from chilling. The thermal battery could get charged whenever energy from the sun was available, while the refrigeration cycle operated independently,' observes Chandramogan. In October 2007, while on a visit to Chicago to meet with the non-resident investor Kirtikant Shah, he flew down to Boston. Sam White and Sorin Grama had invited him to deliver a lecture to management students at the Harvard Business School on 'Indian agriculture and the role of Hatsun'. On October 20, Chandramogan wrote a cheque of $ 5,000 for the techies to develop their solar-powered thermal battery-based chilling system. For the next two years or more, they spent designing and building it at their workshop in Boston. Chandramogan didn't hear much from them, nor did they approach him for any fresh funding.

Around February 2011, Grama and White had their milk chiller ready to be shipped out. Chandramogan had beforehand offered that they could install and test it out at HAP's Karumapuram dairy. The two stayed for two or three months at the company's guest house in Salem, cooking their own food and living like frugal backpackers. Chandramogan wasn't quite impressed with what he saw after they had finished with the installation. 'Although it chilled effectively, the equipment with all the solar panels occupied some 300 square feet, which was like adding two new HMBs to an existing one. But I did not want to discourage them. They were passionate about this whole thing and had come to me after doing a lot of groundwork, including interacting with a few other dairy people in India,' he recalls.

Grama and White eventually dispensed with the idea of a solar-powered chiller. Instead, they developed a new thermal battery that stored normal electricity and released that energy to run a refrigeration cycle. They also designed a more compact system capable of storing extra thermal energy in lesser space. The earlier 2,000-litre solar battery could chill only 500 litres of milk. The new 500-litre battery took four to five hours to charge fully. With that single charge, it chilled 650 litres. If grid power was available for a few more hours during this period, it could chill to its full silo capacity of 1,000 litres.

In March 2012, HAP converted its first HMB at Mottur in Dharmapuri district's Harur *taluka* into an Active Bulk Cooler or ABC system. The milk from there earlier was going to a chilling centre at Kambainallur, 30 km away. The ABC was essentially an HMB equipped with a milk chiller manufactured and installed by Promethean Spenta Technologies, the Pune-based company that Grama and White had founded. Over the next few years, HAP gave this start-up a lot of business by converting many of its HMBs to ABCs. By 2015–16, out of the total 7,896 HMBs, 107 were ABCs. At the end of 2019–20, HAP had 9,101 HMBs, out of which 953 were ABCs. The silo or milk tank of an ABC had a capacity of 1,000 litres, and around 650 litres of milk collected in the morning could be chilled with a single battery charge. Once that was taken away by the milk tanker, another 650 litres could be chilled in the evening, making it possible to do 1,300 litres with two liftings. That included milk from the ABC itself, plus another three or four HMBs within a 4-km radius.

The ABCs resulted in a marked improvement in milk quality. The milk collected could be cooled from 35 degrees to 4 degrees Celsius within an hour or hour and a half. Not only did that bring down the bacterial count, but there were also cost savings. Milk from a normal HMB had to be transported in 35-litre aluminium cans to a chilling centre and unloaded there. After chilling, it needed to be loaded again for dispatch to the dairy. In the ABS, there was no requirement of cans costing Rs 3,500 or so. The tankers had pipes that could be connected to a pump in the milk cooling tank. The milk was pumped into the tanker and taken straight to the dairy, thus saving primary transport, handling and can costs.

In July 2017, HAP set up an 'ABC+' system at Hamsabhavi village in Hirekerur *taluka* of Karnataka's Haveri district that supplied to the Shiralakoppa chilling centre. The ABC+ had the same thermal storage system along with a generator backup. This enabled the chiller to operate to its full 1,000-litres capacity even if there was no power to re-charge the battery simultaneously with its releasing energy. Thus, 2,000 litres could now be chilled in two liftings. Out of HAP's 953 ABCs installed by 2019–20, 421 were ABC+ systems.

The ABCs—with their thermal battery, chilling unit, cooling tank and other parts—cost Rs 12 lakh each. The gen-sets in the ABC+ raised it to Rs 14 lakh. At an average of Rs 11 lakh since the first installation in March 2012, the cumulative expenditure by HAP in these has been roughly Rs 105 crore. Like the Ekomilk analysers and rooftop solar panels in HMBs costing Rs 115 crore, the systems for direct milk procurement and payment to farmer accounts, the fodder development, animal husbandry services and cow tagging programmes, this has been yet another investment with an eye on the long term.

Value chain compression

We have seen how HAP, from the mid-2000s, had replaced its earlier milk marketing system, via a chain of super-stockists and Arokya exclusive retailers, with Hatsun Distribution Centres or HDCs. The HDCs, many of them erstwhile Arokya exclusive retailers, were billed directly by the company and supplied 'Arokya' milk and 'Hatsun' curd to provision stores/retail outlets in their respective areas. In December 2013, the HDC experiment was extended to ice cream. That month, the first Company Direct Store or CDS was opened at Nellore in Andhra Pradesh. Like the HDCs in milk and curd, the CDSs stocked 'Arun' ice cream sourced directly from HAP's factory and supplied it to regular retail stores.

'The franchisee model of only parlours selling 'Arun' ice cream, which we had developed in the 1980s, was unique and novel for that time. But it was getting outdated, with the franchisees themselves ageing. Although the Arun exclusive parlours count rose to about 1,050 by 2004, they had fallen to hardly 850 in early-2010. The model that once served us very well became a constraint to expanding our sales. Also, starting new parlours was a challenge, given rising rentals and parking problems,' says Sathyan. He, along with Thanarajan, was now looking after much of the company's backend and frontend operations, with Chandramogan focusing on overall finance, planning and strategy.

From around February 2010, HAP began supplying 'Arun Exclusive Cabinets'—400-litre deep-freezers stocking only ice cream—to retail outlets through its depots and distributors.

The AECs were placed at provision stores, bakeries, supermarkets and even the HDCs. In the process, retailing of 'Arun' ice cream was opened up for non-franchisees. By January 2015, the number of 'Arun' exclusive parlours had reduced to 430 and further to 246 as of end-March 2020. Once the HDC model was extended to ice cream from end-2013, the company started supplying straight to the CDSs, rendering the stockists/distributors redundant. The CDSs directly stocked ice cream from the plant and supplied not only to the AECs kept in various retail outlets, but also to the 'Arun' exclusive parlours.

Towards the middle of the decade, the HDCs and CDSs were re-branded as Hatsun Daily-Fresh (HD-Fresh) and Hatsun Daily-Long Life (HD-LL) stores, respectively. The first HD-Fresh store was opened on 19 November 2014 at Velachery in south Chennai, while the maiden HD-LL outlet came up in the commercial neighbourhood of Royapettah on 26 December 2015.

Each with 250–350 square feet space, the HD-Fresh stores typically stocked pouch milk and curd in two 500-litres capacity coolers. These came from HAP's dairy by refrigerated trucks to a transit point—usually a fuel filling station or open ground—for the HD-Fresh franchisee to pick up in his own 1–2 tonne polyurethane foam-insulated container vehicle. He delivered the bulk of this to the retail outlets in his area while keeping the balance at the HD-Fresh store to meet on-demand or emergency supplies. Apart from the two coolers dedicated to retailers, the franchisee had a separate visi-cooler (for stocking milk, curd, butter, ghee, *paneer*, flavoured milk, whey drink and other products) and a display freezer (for ice cream). These, of 400–450 litres capacity each, were meant exclusively for counter sales. Roughly 90 per cent of an HD-Fresh store's sales were to retailers and the rest to consumers buying from its counter.

The HD-LL stores were bigger in size (600–800 square feet) with about ten 500-litres capacity deep-freezers to stock ice cream for supplying to the AECs in retail points. In their case, the reefer vehicle from HAP's plant delivered the product (maintained at about minus 18 degrees Celsius, as against 4–5 degrees for milk or curd) straight to the store. The HD-LL franchisee, in turn, put the ice cream in polyurethane foam bags containing freeze pads inside and carried these by two-wheeler to the retail outlets. The HD-LL stores also had two or three separate display freezers and a visi-cooler, 400–500 litres each, for counter sales of ice cream and fresh products, respectively. At an average 15 per cent, the proportion of such sales was higher than for HD-Fresh stores.

'The new distribution model has given us more flexibility in retailing our products, especially ice cream that is now placed in AECs of 100, 300, 400, 500 and 600 litres. Since 2018, 'Arun' ice cream is also being sold through 50-litre deep-freezers, which we are calling Arun Mini Exclusive Cabinets or AMECs. These mini-freezers can be kept in small corner stores and even *pan* shops to stock our Little Bites, Blox and Sandwich ice creams, whose price points, from Rs 5 to Rs 20, compete with toffees or biscuits. Alongside expanding our retail reach, we have compressed the distribution value chain. The milk and ice cream from the plants go only to the HD-Fresh and HD-LL stores. The clearing & forwarding agent's job is to simply transport the product from the plant to these stores. They handle the entire stocking and distribution to retailers,' points out Sathyan.

In 2014–15, there were 31 HD-Fresh stores; by 2019–20, they had swelled to 2,447. Similarly, the number of HD-LL outlets rose from 36 in 2015-16 to 533 in 2019–20. In the process, the HDCs, which peaked at 1,814 in 2014–15, had reduced to 278 five years later, with the CDS count also falling from 137 to 14 between 2016–17 and 2019–20. 'They will all be converted to HD-Fresh and HD-LL stores by 2021-end,' adds Sathyan. The rent and electricity for these stores is paid by HAP, which also supplies the visi-coolers, display freezers and AECs/AMECs, to their and others' retail counters. The franchisees only invest in the deep freezers and insulated vehicles used for stocking and distributing the company's products to retailers.

'We are probably India's only dairy concern to transport packed milk and curd in refrigerated trucks, as opposed to mere insulated tankers, from our plants. A product loaded at 4–5 degrees Celsius in a refrigerated truck retains that temperature all through, whereas this will rise to 8 degrees or so after three hours in normal insulated vehicles. Moving fresh products in refrigerated condition, until the transit points where the HD franchisees take delivery, costs us about 20 paise more per litre. But it is an investment, similar to the ABCs that we have installed at our HMBs, for maintaining quality and end-to-end cold chain integrity. We are able to incur the extra cost mainly due to our hub-and-spoke model of having dairies in multiple locations, which helps bring down both the travel distance and time,' stresses Chandramogan.

The 3,272 HD-Fresh, HD-LL, HD and CDS stores—servicing almost 2 lakh, mostly mom-and-pop, retailers—employ five people on an average, including the staff making daily deliveries on two-wheelers. Together with the two or three persons in each of the 632 'Arun,' 'Ibaco' and 'Oyalo' exclusive outlets (more on the latter two brands in the next chapter), they would add up to nearly 18,000. The 9,101 procurement centres engage another 10,000-odd people, assuming one person for every HMB and two in ABCs. Then, there are the 5,400-plus vehicles deployed for procuring milk, delivering products from plants to stores directly (HD-LL) or via transit points (HD-Fresh), and also transporting feed, ingredients and other raw materials. At an average of 110 km, these vehicles together traverse almost 600,000 km daily, equivalent to going around the earth fifteen times! Moreover, each of them provides daily work to one driver and one helper/cleaner, or roughly 10,000 people. Finally, HAP has some 10,500 employees, about 5,000 on permanent rolls and the remaining on fixed-term contracts.

'If you take all these 48,000–49,000 people, along with the 3.8 lakh farmers pouring milk, ours is a Corporate Social Enterprise. It is a company owned by shareholders, but with far many more stakeholders than one would expect from a private corporate enterprise. Corporate Social Enterprise is an appropriate description for Hatsun,' states Chandramogan.

That partly also has to do with the very nature of dairying as a business. 'How many industries do we know, where the producer gets 60 per cent of the price paid by the consumer? Besides, is there any product that is as fast-moving as milk and allows small mom-and-pop stores to rotate their capital 365 times a year?' he asks.

A shopkeeper selling 40 litres of milk daily at Rs 50/litre gets back the Rs 2,000 money invested, plus a margin of Rs 80 at 4 per cent, on the very same day. The cumulative return on a daily rotating capital of Rs 2,000 at the end of one month, then, is Rs 2,400 or 120 per cent! The capital rotation period may be only slightly longer—say, a day and a half—for curd. Ultimately, it is items such as milk, curd, bread and eggs that keep India's ordinary *kirana* stores going, even with small margins on fast-rotating capital.

Chandramogan gives credit to Verghese Kurien's 'Amul' cooperative model for pioneering the direct collection of milk from lakhs of farmers for processing and marketing to urban consumers. HAP has followed this model but improved upon it by emphasizing lowering production costs at the farm and cutting down middlemen even for making payments. While raising the income and welfare of the farming community is a most desirable goal, the right way to achieve it is not through blindly increasing procurement prices that would only erode the global competitiveness of the Indian dairy industry. Instead, it is by making them more productive and cost-efficient. By directly engaging with the farmer (B2F) and selling branded products that are consumer-facing (B2C), as opposed to commodities (B2B), Hatsun has created a B2F-B2C model unique in itself.

6

New Horizons

It took roughly eighteen years for R.G. Chandramogan's business to achieve annual sales of Rs one crore (in 1987–88) and another thirteen years to cross Rs 100 crore (in 2000–01). But the Rs 1,000 crore-plus mark was reached in just the next eight years (2008–09). That time frame further halved to four years for Rs 2,000 crore (2012–13), another four for Rs 4,000 crore (2016–17) and three years for Rs 5,000 crore (2019–20). For the year ended 31 March 2020, HAP recorded a profit after tax of Rs 112.27 crore on net sales of Rs 5,308.33 crore.

HAP's becoming a Rs 5,000 crore-plus company fittingly came just before it turned fifty on 7 April 2020. This was a journey that had seen it traverse every stage an enterprise could potentially have: starting from tiny (1970s) and small (early 1980s), to medium (late-eighties onwards), big (mid-2000s) and finally large (post-2015).

As Chandramogan succinctly puts it, 'The combined turnover of my first ten years wasn't even Rs 25 lakh, which HAP now grosses in below 25 minutes. Our cumulative sales over the first twenty and thirty years would, likewise, have been about Rs 12 crore and Rs 450 crore, which we, during 2019–20, did in less than a day and just over a month, respectively. The Rs 5,308.33 crore of last fiscal was furthermore equal to our sales over the first forty years'. And all this was from an initial equity capital of Rs 13,000 mobilized through selling a portion of ancestral property in his hometown!

The above growth was driven by investments, both in production capacities and brand-building. HAP's gross fixed assets—the value of plant and machinery, land, buildings, furniture and fixtures, office equipment, vehicles, etc. at original cost—increased from a mere Rs 34.65 crore in 2000–01 to Rs 499.54 crore in 2010–11 and Rs 2,434.55 crore in 2019–20. The investments, in turn, were largely funded through debt. As we saw in chapter 3, HAP's total secured and unsecured loans, between 1999–2000 and 2009–10, rose from Rs 10.86 crore to Rs 313.74 crore, with the latter nearly six times the company's share capital and reserves. Even in 2017–18, when borrowings peaked at Rs 1,298.95 crore, these were 3.55 times the shareholders' funds of Rs 365.53 crore.

'I will readily admit that my company has grown with bankers' money. But that money has been primarily used for investing in milk processing, procurement and associated infrastructure. We have hardly borrowed for working capital, as our raw material (milk) is obtained from farmers on ten-days' credit, while the company's products are sold wholly on a cash-and-carry basis. So, even when our debt-equity ratios were high, we rarely faced liquidity problems that come with huge trade receivables or products not moving fast enough. That's why banks have been comfortable financing us. By regularly discharging interest, I have effectively acted as an executive taking care of their investments,' says Chandramogan in a lighter vein. In 2019–20, HAP's interest outgo, at Rs 82.73 crore, was only 1.56 per cent of its net sales.

The company, however, did undertake periodic equity infusions to reassure lenders. The first such infusion, it would be recalled, took place in July 2009, via the issue of unsecured compulsorily convertible debentures to a few high net worth investors for a total value of Rs 25 crore. The allotment of equity shares against these happened in December 2010. A similar preferential issue of shares to select non-promoter investors followed in November 2014, which was for an aggregate consideration of Rs 30 crore—again with a view to shore up HAP's equity base. In June 2018, the company came out with a rights issue to existing shareholders for an amount aggregating Rs 527.83 crore. Out of the proceeds, about Rs 524 crore was used to repay and also prepay some bank loans. This issue was a wholly voluntary exercise to pare debt sans pressure from banks, unlike in the earlier two fund infusions. As a result, on 31 March 2020, HAP's total borrowings had come down to Rs 1,197.02 crore, while only 1.32 times the shareholders' funds of Rs 904.48 crore (Rs 16.17 crore share capital and Rs 888.31 crore reserves & surplus).

The strategy of relying on bank borrowings for financing investments—significantly enabled by the company virtually operating on negative working capital—has also translated into better rewards for HAP's shareholders. Since the time its previous avatar Hatsun Milk Food Ltd made an initial public offer (IPO) in January 1996, the company's paid-up equity capital has expanded very little: from Rs 5 crore to Rs 21.56 crore. The gains would have been huge for the investor who subscribed to the IPO at Rs 45/share, both from price appreciation and stock splits-cum-bonus issues.

On 24 July 2008, each 10-rupee HAP share got split into five shares of Rs 2 face value. On 4 October 2011, there was a further stock split, so that the original one share of Rs 10 now became ten shares of one-rupee face value each. The company, in addition, came out with bonus share issues—one for every existing two on 27 March 2012, two for every five on 14 July 2016 and one for every three on 10 December 2020. At the end of the day, there were twenty-eight HAP shares from the original one share bought at Rs 45 by the IPO investor. Given HAP's share price of Rs 893.75 at end-June 2021 at the Bombay Stock Exchange, the effective appreciation (Rs 25,025 over Rs 45) worked out to 55,511 per cent!

What is more, the investor would have received dividend income on the shares held. There were no years, barring 2001–02 and 2004–05 when the company did not declare dividends. The 800 per cent dividend (Rs 8 on 21 one-rupee shares) paid for 2019–20 would have been equal to Rs 168 on the original Rs 10 share subscribed at Rs 45.

By growing using bank money, the company could ensure minimal equity dilution, hence better returns to existing shareholders, and retain a relatively high stake for the promoters. Chandramogan and his family held 74.07 per cent in HAP, which had a total market capitalization (the value of its publicly-listed shares) of Rs 19,266 crore as of 30 June 2021. The stable management that ensued has made it possible for the company to not be subjected to quarterly earnings pressures and, instead, undertake investments yielding returns in the long run. That included—apart from EKO HMBs, ABCs, fodder development and veterinary support, and the distribution value chain compression through Hatsun Daily stores—brand building. HAP's expenditure on advertisement and sales promotion in 2019–20 amounted to Rs 104.73 crore.

'We have been spending year after year on brand building, which does not get reflected as an asset on our balance sheet. In reality, it is our most precious asset. While gross block or fixed assets matter, the true strength of any FMCG company lies in its brands. If I am only producing commodity milk powder, raising prices isn't easy, as others selling the same undifferentiated thing will simply grab my market share. In contrast, a 5 per cent upward price revision in Arokya milk or Arun ice cream wouldn't lead to overnight switching by consumers. Multinationals acquire Indian companies for their brands, not factories and other physical assets. Even banks know it is safer lending to firms that generate cash flow from products having strong brand equity,' notes Chandramogan.

Integrating backwards...

Unlike most FMCG companies, including multinationals, HAP has eschewed contract manufacturing. It has, instead, consistently strived for 'making itself' and seeking maximum backward integration. This was seen first in ice cream, where it went for sourcing of actual milk, as against powder and cream. Even in milk, the strategy adopted was to go and procure from producers, bypassing all middlemen. This direct engagement with farmers was later on extended to supplying them cattle feed, which again was produced in-house.

In the last ten years, HAP has taken further steps at backward integration. In 2010, about Rs 5 crore was invested to put up wafer cone and chocolate paste making machines at Karumapuram, which had been turned into an ice cream facility after scrapping its liquid milk plant in March 2009. In 2018, a second cone biscuit line, more high-end and costing Rs 20 crore, was added. By manufacturing ice cream cone and chocolate paste on its own, purchases were now restricted only to their raw materials: *maida* (refined wheat flour) and sugar in the former and cocoa mass/ butter for the latter. The company could, then, exercise better control over both cost and quality.

'Transporting cones is expensive, as they occupy more space with lesser weight and also need to be packed in cardboard boxes. Sugar and *maida* can be bought and transported easily. You pay by weight, not volume,' points out Chandramogan. Much before all this, the Nallur, as well as Tollgate factories, had their own bakeries to supply cake for 'Arun' cassata ball and ice cream cake rolls, 'which you could call our first backward integration projects'!

In September 2017, HAP set up an automated plastic film extrusion-cum-flexo printing plant at Walajabad in Kanchipuram. Entailing an investment of Rs 63 crore, with machinery from Windmöller & Hölscher of Germany, it would meet the company's entire requirement of plastic pouches for 'Arokya' milk and 'Hatsun' curd. Pouch manufacturing basically involved melting virgin high-density polyethylene granules and pushing the molten polymer through a die for further shaping. Chandramogan estimates the cost savings from making pouches, as opposed to buying, at a 'minimum 10 per cent'. It also ensured better quality of packaging, which mattered especially for fresh dairy products.

The other significant effort at backward integration has been investments in wind and solar power generation to reduce dependence on electricity purchases from the grid. In March 2017, HAP commissioned twelve wind mills of 24 megawatts (MW) aggregate capacity in Thoothukudi district's Kayathar belt at a cost of Rs 180 crore. The turbine generators, each of 2 MW, were supplied by the Spanish wind power engineering major Gamesa (now Siemens Gamesa Renewable Energy). In addition, the company spent over Rs 14 crore during 2018–19 on erecting solar rooftop installations totalling 3.6 MW—1.05 MW at the Palani feed mill and the rest at the Palacode (1.65 MW), Tirunelveli (0.5 MW), Belgaum (0.2 MW) and Honnali (0.2 MW) dairies. The turnkey contract for these was given to Sun Best, a Theni-based solar services provider.

Since 2018–19, HAP has been generating 5–6 crore units out of its total annual electricity consumption of 9.5–10 crore units from renewable sources. The existing wind turbines and solar panels can, in a full year, potentially produce six crore units and 54 lakh units, respectively. 'Around 60 per cent of the energy consumed by our factories is now being supplied from captive green sources. The aim is to push it up to 75 per cent and bring down reliance on purchase of power, particularly for products such as ice cream,' says Chandramogan, who, even back in 1993, had put up a 250 kilovolt-ampere (200 kilowatt) windmill at Muppandal in Kanyakumari district to meet part of the power requirements of the Ramalingapuram and Tollgate ice cream units. 'It was an NEPC turbine that generated 5–6 lakh units annually. We ran it for twenty-four years, which more than recovered the capital cost of Rs 40 lakh, including land. The mill supplied electricity to the grid, and we could draw equivalent power for our factories by paying a wheeling charge to the state utility,' he adds.

Chandramogan re-emphasizes the long-term nature of all these investments: 'Shareholders chasing quick returns would not have understood the need for HAP to set up its own cone-making or plastic film unit. They would rather have wanted us to declare higher profits and dividends. The investments made will deliver precisely those in the years to come'.

Bank borrowings aside, a key source of financing the investments has been depreciation. During 2015–16 to 2019–20, HAP's cumulative provision for depreciation, at Rs 920.66 crore, has accounted for over 44 per cent of its total earnings before interest, tax and depreciation (EBIDTA) of 2,079.66 crores, while far exceeding interest expenses of Rs 417.66 crore for this period. Depreciation, unlike interest, isn't an outgo and, to the extent it reduces the company's taxable income, is equivalent to a source of cash. 'By providing for high depreciation initially, we keep our tax outflow low. The favourable tax effect may reduce in the later years, but by then, the investments made will start generating higher EBIDTA and profits before tax,' explains Chandramogan.

...and forward

Alongside backward integration has been the focus on forward integration and continuous product upgradation. HAP, we saw, was India's first dairy concern to move packed milk and curd from its plants in refrigerated trucks, as opposed to mere insulated tankers, notwithstanding the extra costs involved. In 2009, the company installed an instant quick freeze (IQF) equipment in its newly-opened Karumapuram ice cream factory and two years later at Nallur. Previously, the already-prepared ice cream in semi-solid form was being taken at 4 degrees Celsius to the cold store and gradually frozen to minus 18 degrees over eight to ten hours. But with the IQF machines—from Denmark's Dantech Freezing Systems—the temperatures were brought down from 4 to minus 25 degrees within forty-five minutes. The product was now moved from there to the cold store, where it would be preserved at minus 18 degrees.

'IQF prevents crystallisation of water particles and ice flake formation. The faster the ice cream freezes, the creamier it will be. Today, 100 per cent of our ice cream is based on IQF. From around 2007, we had started to source emulsifiers and stabilizers from globally renowned companies such as Denmark's Danisco. These again cost more. We have over time also increased the milk fat content in our ice cream to up to 13 per cent (against the mandated 10 per cent) and reduced the air overrun to 70–90 per cent (the standard is 100 per cent),' states Sathyan. Overrun is the amount of air pumped into the ice cream while it is being formed in the continuous freezer. 100 per cent overrun means one part of air being added to every one part of ice cream. The swell from the incorporation of air particles gives a smoother and more velvety texture to the ice cream.

Offering more fat has, of course, been possible only due to HAP being a dairy company having its own direct milk procurement system. The benefits of cost savings, from not buying milk powder and cream from others, have been passed on to consumers by selling ice cream with higher fat content. The better quality of ingredients and superior freezing technology employed has also allowed its ice cream to command a value-for-money premium among consumers. 'We hardly sell to hotels or institutional customers who would demand bulk discounts and material on credit. Even for retail consumers, the last time that we came out with schemes like *oru arai vaangna, oru arai free* (buy half-a-litre and get one half-a-litre free) was back in mid-2000,' avers Sathyan.

In 2010, HAP installed an extrusion machine at Karumapuram. The ice cream now—instead of being put as a semi-frozen liquid into cups, cones or moulds—came out straight through a tube stiffer and colder in different unique shapes: from heart and funny face to teddy bear. 'Some companies like Dinshaw's had tried out extruded ice cream in the early 2000s, but the technology wasn't fully evolved then and the equipment was also expensive. The machine we bought for about Rs one crore was one that a Czech Republic company Vojta had displayed at an exhibition in Mumbai. Subsequently, we invested in three other machines supplied by Tetra Pak (Switzerland) and Gram Equipment (Denmark). These could extrude many more pieces per hour. We are able to offer a range of ice creams—Little Bites, Blox, Sandwich, Whale, Watermelon, Jolly Train, Two-in-One, Trio, Spiral, iBar and even Chocobar—in the extruded form today,' informs Sathyan.

On 21 February 2012, a new product was launched: 'Ibaco'. This was a brand of ice cream sold through exclusive outlets—the first one at Anna Nagar West in Chennai—with two distinguishing characteristics. First, it was based on the scoop-and-serve format. Consumers could walk into an 'Ibaco' store and create their own sundae bar or waffle cone ice cream, by choosing from thiry-six flavours and topping it with assorted dry fruits, nuts, chocolate buttons and sauces. Second, pricing was by weight. Whether they bought blackcurrant, butterscotch, bean vanilla, fresh strawberry, mango or Belgian chocolate, payment was on a flat per-kg basis. The air overrun in 'Ibaco' was also 65–70 per cent, compared to 85–90 per cent for 'Arun' ice cream.

Even before 'Ibaco,' HAP had experimented with scoop-and-serve through an 'Arun Unlimited' store, started on 7 June 2004 at the Spencer Plaza mall in Chennai's Anna Salai (Mount Road). There were forty-seven such outlets by the time 'Ibaco' came into being. All of them were converted into 'Ibaco' stores, whose numbers expanded to 99 by March 2014, 126 by March 2016 and 170 at the end of March 2020. But why a new brand when 'Arun Unlimited' already existed?

Chandramogan has a ready answer: 'We introduced the consumer to real ice cream through Arun. The same consumer now wanted to taste the next level of ice cream. Why should we vacate that space to a Baskin-Robbins or a Häagen-Dazs? Let those who went to Arun school join Ibaco college!'

And where did the name come from?: 'We asked our agency (Rubecon Communications) to think of something that was exotic-sounding, had vowels both at the start and end and also our consumers could easily pronounce. They gave us a few options, from which we chose Ibaco. Even today, many think it is a foreign brand, which has to do with the store ambience and a different product feel'. The consumer buying 'Arun' for Rs 60 per 100 grams didn't mind paying Rs 95–100 for the same quantity of 'Ibaco' ice cream having less overrun and in a totally new setting.

Like in the Hatsun Daily stores, the electricity and rent for the 'Ibaco' stores were paid for by the company itself. The franchisee was, in addition, given monthly sustenance akin to a basic salary and a maintenance allowance for the store's upkeep. On top of these fixed overheads, he received an average 7 per cent commission on the sales value; it ranged from 8 per cent for sales of up to Rs 2.5 lakh per month and 4 per cent beyond Rs 4 lakh. Together, they added up to 26–30 per cent, depending on the store's turnover. 'Most companies pay a flat 30 per cent commission to the franchisee, who may or may not do everything to maintain the product integrity. In our case, the franchisee had no reason to shut off electricity or not run the generator when there were no consumers; we were footing even the diesel bill. The 7 per cent margin was reasonable as we were taking care of the bulk of his overheads,' states Chandramogan.

'Ibaco' took six years to achieve break even—proof of how long and how much effort goes into building a brand. According to Chandramogan, each outlet had to do a minimum average business of Rs 48 lakh for turning EBITDA-positive. That was crossed in 2017–18. The viability of the outlets went up further with sales of 'Ibaco' chocolates. HAP had, in 2017, invested Rs 18 crore in a full-fledged chocolate unit at the Karumapuram plant, with a capacity to produce and pack 125,000 pieces per day. 'We were already making chocolate paste. This was just one step more. Chocolates and ice cream being complementary products, the former could ride on the latter,' he avers.

In August 2019, the London-based market research firm Euromonitor International ranked HAP as India's third-largest ice cream player. It had a market share of 5.5 per cent by value, behind Gujarat Cooperative Milk Marketing Federation's (GCMMF) 17.7 per cent and Hindustan Unilever Ltd's (HUL) 9.2 per cent. HAP had, between 2015–16 and 2018–19, moved up from sixth to third position, leaving behind RJ Corporation, Mother Dairy and Vadilal Industries. Also, 'Arun' was the second-largest independent ice cream brand after GCMMF's 'Amul'—ahead of RJ Corp's 'Cream Bell,' 'Mother Dairy,' 'Vadilal,' Lotte Confectionary's 'Havmor' and HUL's 'Kwality Wall's' and 'Cornetto'. Moreover, HUL sold only frozen desserts that use vegetable oil, not milk fat. HAP was, therefore, a clear No. 2 when it came to real ice cream. And this was despite 'Arun' or 'Ibaco' not getting marketed in north, east and much of western India, unlike 'Amul'.

A more recent addition to HAP's brand stable is 'Oyalo' pizza, launched in April 2017. For Chandramogan, pizza represented yet another forward integration initiative, as more than 50 per cent of its value was accounted for by cheese. Being a dairy company, HAP was already making cheese, similar to not having to purchase skimmed milk powder and cream for its ice cream. And like the extra fat offered on ice cream, 'Oyalo' had 30 per cent cheese content by weight, against 25 per cent in normal pizzas. 'Oyalo' pizza was also to be produced in HAP's own ready-to-eat factory at Guduvanchery in Chengalpattu district, about 40 km from Chennai. The dough used as base was made there, the cheese, tomatoes and vegetables added, and the pizza cooked in an oven before being frozen and supplied to the 'Oyalo' outlets. The outlet franchisee had to simply take it out from the freezer and reheat in his oven to serve consumers. By March 2020, there were 216 'Oyalo' outlets. In October 2019, a second ready-to-eat factory was opened at Noyyal, which previously housed a cattle feed unit and then an ice cream store. The Guduvanchery facility, started in December 2014 on hired premises, was eventually shut.

But the most successful of HAP's forward integration products, on which we haven't focussed much, has been curd. The product, as already seen, was first launched in 2001 under the 'Dairy Choice' brand and then re-launched as 'Hatsun' curd by 2005-end. But even at the start of the next decade, the company's curd sales were hardly 15,000–20,000 kg per day, and it was being produced from the Ramalingapuram, Palacode, Thimmasamudram and Belgaum dairies. In April 2013, a dedicated 100,000-kg per day plant was opened at Vellichandai, which had earlier served as a 'Sikkanam' packing godown. That was when the volumes began to surge. HAP's daily sales of curd now average over 3.5 lakh kg, with the revenues from it competing with ice cream.

'Our approach all through has been to identify products that people were making at home and which they may be prepared to buy. We experimented with cooking butter and sweetened *khoa*, which failed. Curd clicked because it was a product that the consumer, having bought once, didn't go back to making at home. While curd might eat a little into milk sales, it could still ride on the latter's marketing network. In that sense, they were complementary products, just as chocolates and ice cream or cattle feed and milk procurement,' notes Chandramogan.

The initial marketing campaign around curd highlighted the convenience factor—targeting the working woman, virtually asking whether she had the time to set curd. Subsequently, it spoke about quality—how 'Hatsun' curd maintained the same taste, flavour and consistency across all weather conditions, unlike homemade curd that didn't form properly during the winter or rainy season. 'The starter cultures used in our curd were imported from France, Denmark and Italy, which we still do. This, together with the fresh quality of milk collected by us, ensured that the product also scored in spoonability and the right amount of sourness,' says Sathyan.

'Hatsun' curd was made from toned milk, though it had more than the usual 3 per cent fat and 8.5 per cent solids-not-fats (SNF) content. In February 2015, 'Arokya' curd was introduced. This one was positioned as a curd close to what was made at home from milk. The milk here, needless to add, was 'Arokya' milk. 'Arokya' curd was predictably thicker and creamier, with both standardized (4.5 per cent fat and 8.5 per cent SNF) and full-cream (6 per cent fat and 9 per cent SNF) milk versions.

Meanwhile, milk itself—which continues to be the company's mainstay, contributing well over 60 per cent of its net sales, as against curd's 12 per cent and ice cream's 11 per cent—saw a change. HAP had originally carved out a niche with 'Naalarai Paal,' as its standardized milk came to be known. But over time, 'Arokya' became more of a full-cream milk brand. Out of the roughly 20 lakh litres per day 'Arokya' milk sales today, almost 60 per cent comprises full-cream, with standardized at 30 per cent and low-fat making up the balance. 'The Indian consumer's preference is generally for milk with higher fat. The reason for it could be flexibility. With full-cream milk, you can dilute the fat content by simply adding water. The reverse, of increasing the fat content in milk having less cream, isn't possible. We have merely anticipated and followed the consumer,' sums up Chandramogan.

The ultimate proof of HAP being a retail consumer-focussed company is that the B2B segment generates hardly 2.5 per cent of the company's sales. Even its institutional buyers are mostly the likes of Ferrero, which is willing to pay more for quality dairy ingredients used in its own premium chocolate and confectionery products.

Beyond TN

Raju Chandrakant Kharade, till three years ago, had only a home, nine buffaloes and no land to farm at Kamti Budruk village in Mohol *taluka* of Maharashtra's Solapur district. The thirty-one-year-old made a living by selling milk from his buffaloes in Solapur city, besides cooking meals at marriages and other social functions. Around mid-2018, he bought a one-acre plot in the neighbouring village of Wagholi for Rs 12.5 lakh using his accumulated savings. Further, he purchased nine Holstein crossbred cows for Rs 4.5 lakh, funded mainly through the sale of seven of his nine buffaloes.

Today, Kharade supplies 90 litres of milk daily to HAP's Active Bulk Cooler (ABC) at Wagholi. This village not only has an ABC but two Hatsun Milk Banks (HMB) as well. The first HMB was opened in September 2016 and the second one in February 2017, while the ABC itself came up in February 2018. From a mere 120 litres to start with, the company's average collection per day from Wagholi has risen to 4,500 litres, of which 2,200 litres is through the ABC and the remaining from the two HMBs.

'I bought land and replaced most of my buffaloes with cows only because of Hatsun. They have a transparent system of payment based on fat and SNF, and the money comes straight to my bank account,' says Kharade, who also grows CoFS-29 hybrid sorghum fodder on his entire one-acre land.

Forty-year-old Somnath Giram, unlike Kharade, is an original inhabitant of Wagholi. He is more prosperous, owning 35 acres jointly with four brothers. They cultivate sugarcane and *jowar* (sorghum) on 10 acres each, onion on five acres, and CoFS-29 and fodder maize on the remaining 10 acres. His family also pours about 100 litres of milk from twelve cows to HAP. 'We had nineteen cows till 2015, which fell to three by early-2017. Our milk was bought by bulk vendors who supplied it to other dairies. When prices crashed to Rs 15–18 per litre and payments weren't being made for seventy to eighty days even at these rates, we had to dispose of the cows that once cost Rs 80,000–90,000 for Rs 20,000–25,000 each,' states Giram, who is now guaranteed a minimum Rs 25-per-litre price. Like in all the HMBs of HAP, his milk is tested on an Ekomilk analyser and electronically weighed, with details of the quantity poured, the rate corresponding to the fat-SNF content of the tested sample and the payment due all displayed in front of Giram. And the money, too, is regularly credited every ten days.

HAP began procuring milk from Maharashtra on 10 January 2015. From day one, it was bought directly from farmers, unlike of other dairies that entrusted the job to bulk vendors. The latter typically charged a Rs 2–2.50/litre commission for aggregating milk from the village and transporting it to the dairy's chilling centre. Each vendor, dealing with 50–100 farmers, would also extend advances to them and adjust these against the value of milk supplied. 'When we entered, farmers were getting Rs 17–18 for a standard litre of cow milk with 3.5 per cent fat and 8.5 per cent SNF. We offered to pay Rs 22–23 for the same milk then. But our higher rate, partly due to savings on vendor commission, was conditional on no advances being given. The farmer had to choose between advance and low price or high price and no advance,' observes Chandramogan.

The first HMBs were established in seven villages supplying a chilling centre at Sangola in Solapur district. By November 2015,

HAP, which initially paid farmers daily in cash, had switched to transferring money to their bank accounts once every ten days. 'Some of us heard about this company that was giving a higher price and also paying on time. We, then, went to Patkhal (in Solapur's Mangalvedhe *taluka*, where HAP had opened its second chilling centre) and requested them to start collection from our village,' states Kharade, who is planning to expand his herd size to fifty cows in the next one year.

Salman Maniyar, a farmer from Kamti Budruk, has only turned to commercial dairying only in the last year. Solapur district has suffered four droughts since 2014. That, in addition to price volatility and delayed payments from sugar mills, has made cultivation of grapes and sugarcane a risky proposition. Maniyar grows both crops on half of his 10-acre holding. Maniyar, in April 2020, bought two cows, one for Rs 50,000 and the other for Rs 60,000. He is currently supplying 30 litres from them daily to HAP. These cows have delivered two calves that are already six months old and poised to yield milk in about one and a half years. Like Kharade and Giram, Maniyar has sourced seeds of CoFS-29 fodder sorghum for cultivating on one acre. All of them also buy 'Santosa XL' premium cattle feed of HAP having 25 per cent crude protein content. 'When we are being paid more for milk with higher fat and SNF content, doesn't it make sense to give our cows quality feed and fodder?' he quips.

HAP, we may recall, had ventured beyond TN first by commissioning a dairy at Belgaum in 2000 and a second one at Honnali in 2007, besides unsuccessfully experimenting with selling in markets such as Kolkata. In November 2013, the company acquired the assets of Jyothi Dairy Pvt. Ltd. These included two plants of 65,000 litres-per-day milk processing capacity each at Suraram, near Hyderabad, and Bandapalli in Chittoor district of Andhra Pradesh. The deal cost Rs 50 crore. Another Rs 15 crore was spent towards expanding the capacities of both dairies to 2 lakh litres per day (LLPD) each.

'The promoter (Balaji Tammineedi) approached me, and we finalized the transaction within fifteen days after Sathyan had seen the facilities. They were doing an annual turnover of about Rs 100 crore, procuring 70,000-odd litres daily through bulk vendors and selling mainly to tea shops and institutional customers under their 'Jyothi' brand. For us, the attraction lay in the location of the plants. Further, we recognized that sales in TN were bound to slow down, and growth could only come from new markets. This acquisition was a good way to go about it,' says Chandramogan.

HAP was already selling 'Arokya' milk in AP markets such as Chittoor, Tirupati and Nellore from its Thimmasamudram dairy. The taken-over and expanded Chittoor plant could now supply to these markets as well as other Rayalaseema region towns (Madanapalle, Anantapur, Guntakal, Cuddapah and Kurnool) and Ongole. Likewise, the Hyderabad dairy could cater to Hyderabad and northern Telangana markets like Warangal, Karimnagar and Nizamabad.

'Our forte has always been identifying and developing markets that don't interest others; they only want to sell in the big cities. Also, we have used our existing dairies to seed new markets: for example, Chittoor by Thimmasamudram, Madurai by Karumapuram and Tirunelveli by Madurai. Later on, these markets have been handed over to the newly-commissioned dairies in the same locations, making them viable from day one,' adds Chandramogan.

HAP's expanding milk collection operations to Maharashtra was, in fact, initially prompted by the need to supply to the new Hyderabad plant. The availability of cow milk wasn't too good in Hyderabad and surrounding areas. Most dairies there sourced a mix of buffalo and cow milk. 'Arokya,' on the other hand, was an exclusively full-cream/standardized cow milk brand. Chandramogan was clear that his company wouldn't deal with buffalo milk. Its prices were volatile due to large lean-flush seasonal supply variations and the animals producing less, along with taking longer time to calve, than cows. For feeding the Hyderabad market, it was decided to supplement supplies from Maharashtra's Solapur belt. By April 2016, HAP was procuring from the neighbouring Sangli district as well. Soon, it began selling 'Arokya' milk and 'Hatsun' curd in both places and other Maharashtra markets such as Satara, Pune, Latur and Nanded. In November 2020, HAP also entered the Navi Mumbai market by opening an HD-Fresh store at Kharghar.

During 2019–20, HAP's milk procurement from Maharashtra averaged 2.11 LLPD, of which 1.36 LLPD was from Solapur and 75,000 litres from Sangli. In June 2019, it took over a 100 tonnes-per-day cattle feed unit of Madhur Pashu Aahar, a partnership firm belonging to a doctor couple, at Chandolewadi in Solapur's Sangola *taluka* for Rs 3.56 crore. The real big-ticket investment in Maharashtra was, however, to come just over a year later.

At the start of 2020–21, fifty years after Chandramogan had embarked upon his entrepreneurial journey, HAP had twelve dairies with an aggregate milk handling capacity of 49.75 LLPD.

These included eight in TN: Palacode (15 LLPD, including a 72 tonnes-per-day milk powder plant), Thimmasamudram (9.6 LLPD, including a 1.2 LLPD curd and 12 tonnes-per-day powder facility), Thalaivasal (5.05 LLPD, including 0.7 LLPD of curd), Vadipatti (3.2 LLPD), Karumapuram (25 tonnes-per-day of powder equivalent to 2.5 LLPD), Vellichandai (1.25 LLPD of curd), Ramalingapuram (0.50 LLPD, including a 5-tonnes per day *paneer*-making facility) and Tirunelveli (2.7 LLPD, including 0.6 LLPD of curd). The last-mentioned plant at Poolam village of Tirunelveli's Nanguneri *taluka* came up in July 2014.

The four dairies outside TN were Belgaum (2.2 LLPD, including 0.6 LLPD of curd), Honnali (2.4 LLPD), Chittoor (3 LLPD, including one LLPD of curd) and Hyderabad (2.35 LLPD, including 0.35 LLPD of curd). In addition to the twelve dairies were the two ice cream plants at Karumapuram and Nallur, with respective capacities of 90,000 litres and 40,000 litres per day, and two cattle feed units at Palani (900 tonnes/day) and Sangola (100 tonnes). HAP also has a pizza/ready-to-eat factory at Noyyal and a plastic pouch manufacturing unit at Walajabad.

In 2020–21, the year of the great coronavirus pandemic and a nationwide economic lockdown, two more projects got commissioned. The first one was a Rs 135-crore dairy at Shirashi village in Solapur's Mangalvedhe *taluka*. With a capacity to handle 6 LLPD (2.5 LLPD for pouch milk, 1.5 LLPD for curd and 2 LLPD for concentration), the plant, built on 3 out of a total 70-acre land, marked HAP's true commitment to Maharashtra. The market for it had already been 'seeded' by the company's existing Belgaum facility. Milk from Sangli no longer had to go to Belgaum for processing and bringing back for selling in Satara or Pune. The second one was a 3 LLPD dairy costing Rs 90 crore at Uthiyur near Dharapuram in Tiruppur district of Tamil Nadu. It also housed a five tonnes-per-day *paneer* manufacturing facility, similar to that at Ramalingapuram. Both projects were up and running by January-February 2021.

A third project was HAP's biggest-ever investment—a Rs 311-crore ice cream plant at Govindpur Thanda in Zaheerabad taluka of Telangana's Sangareddy district. Located in a 113-acre campus, its capacity of 1.60 LLPD is more than Karumapuram and Nallur combined. This plant, India's most state-of-the-art, if not largest, will go into production during the third quarter of 2021–22.

For Chandramogan, his business journey has been not about building 20 plants as much as 'touching many people's lives'. They include farmers, employees, trade channel partners, investors and, not the least, consumers. Even as a 74 per cent owner of a Rs 5,500 crore-plus company with over Rs 19,000 crore market capitalization, he wears his wealth lightly. 'All this is notional wealth. I don't consider myself to be a billionaire. In fact, the only asset I have is a house,' Chandramogan told *Forbes India* in its issue dated 20 November 2020. The magazine ranked him the 100th richest Indian in its 2020 list. But Chandramogan puts his company's wealth and interest above himself. He is what he is only because of HAP!

7

The Lockdown

When demonetization happened on 8 November 2016, HAP and its farmers, we saw, 'slept peacefully'. The company had, more than a year before, gone fully cashless in making payments to farmers. Everyone—farmers, employees, transporters and other service providers—were now being paid through direct bank transfers. The HD distributors and 'Ibaco' franchisees, even if they undertook cash transactions with provision store owners and retail consumers, had to credit their collections to HAP's bank account. Nobody in their wildest dreams imagined any government would overnight render invalid 86 per cent of the value of the country's currency notes in circulation. But HAP, by design or serendipity, was prepared and suffered no major disruptions in its operations from demonetization.

That wasn't the case, though, when, on the night of 24 March 2020, Prime Minister Narendra Modi declared a three-week-long nationwide lockdown to contain the spread of COVID-19, the disease caused by a new coronavirus designated as SARS-CoV-2. From that midnight and for the next twenty-one days, there was to be a 'complete ban' on people stepping out of their homes.

'Every state of the country, every union territory, every district, every municipality, every village, every street, every locality is being put under lockdown...Forget what going out means for the next twenty-one days. Stay inside your home,' the Prime Minister stated.

The suddenness of the announcement and its scope notwithstanding, the lockdown decision, unlike demonetization, wasn't something entirely unexpected. Only a couple of days earlier, on 22 March, a 'Janata Curfew'—of people voluntarily remaining indoors for the whole day from 7.00 a.m. to 9.00 p.m.—had been observed across the country. Even prior to that, the Tamil Nadu government, on 16 March, had ordered the closure of schools, colleges, malls, theatres, clubs, bars, tourist resorts, amusement parks, swimming pools, gyms, museums and zoos till 31 March.

'Our antennas had already gone up by 19 March, the day the Prime Minister made the Janata Curfew announcement. We knew this was only a trailer and something more drastic would follow,' recounts Sathyan, who, on 17 March, was with a friend at a Starbucks coffee shop in BSR Mall. Around 11.00 a.m., officials from the Chennai Municipal Corporation came to this mall in Thoraipakkam on the Old Mahabalipuram Road. The mall manager was told in no uncertain terms to obey the state government's instructions issued the previous night. All stores inside had to shut; nobody, except the watchman, could be on the mall premises. For Sathyan, that incident was the shape of things to come. The social distancing measures to prevent the transmission of COVID-19—first reported as 'pneumonia of unknown cause' from China's Wuhan City on 31 December 2019 and declared as a 'global pandemic' by the World Health Organization (WHO) on 11 March—would only get stricter.

Well before even the Janata Curfew, HAP's management had directed all production units to stock up enough fuel (coal, wood and diesel for gensets), water (in tanks), plastic film and other packing material. These were protocols the company had evolved while dealing with past disruptions, including of vehicular movement, in the aftermath of the former TN chief minister J. Jayalalithaa's demise in December 2016 and the mega bandhs resulting from the 2013 move to carve a new Telangana state out of Andhra Pradesh. Stocking up aside, employees were asked not to take leaves or travel out and be available for any contingency. Plant heads and staff were to be close to their factories and the sales and procurement people, likewise, at their assigned reporting locations. Employees could also, wherever it was feasible in order to reduce the numbers at offices, take their laptops to set up and work from home. Much of this was done by 21 March, the Janata Curfew day being a Sunday. Ongoing construction work at the new Shirashi dairy and Govindpur Thanda ice cream factory sites was stopped on 18 March and 20 March, respectively.

In short, unlike demonetization that came like a bolt from the blue, the lockdown wasn't something totally unanticipated.

Cold shock

But the lockdown's impact on HAP was far more serious. For starters, as Sathyan admits, 'We never thought there would be a twenty-one-day lockdown'. Forced confinement to homes for two to three days, daily night curfews, extended flight and rail travel bans were all within the realm of possibility for breaking the chain of infection; twenty-one days was beyond anyone's remotest expectations. It was a challenge that had to be managed nonetheless, with Sathyan taking full charge. Chandramogan and his wife had, on 23 March, left for Thiruthangal. They were seen to be more at risk of contracting the virus and also transmitting it to others. Being away from Chennai in his hometown was considered a safer option. They were to remain in Thiruthangal till 14 April.

The business most affected by the lockdown was ice cream, whose consumption normally peaked during mid-March to mid-June, coinciding with summer vacations for schools. Sales of 'Arun,' however, had started falling from early-March itself in response to rising cases of COVID-19 worldwide. This was compounded by fears, sans any scientific basis, of the infection spreading through eating frozen items (especially ice cream) and chicken (due to past association with bird flu). Between 13 and 20 March, all 'Ibaco' stores shut. On 21 March, a day before the Janata Curfew, the company stopped producing ice cream from both its Karumapuram and Nallur plants. The previous day, it had also suspended operations at the 'Oyalo' pizza/ready-to-eat factory in Guduvanchery. Noyyal ran at minimal capacity till the lockdown formally came into effect.

From 18 March, till the end of the first lockdown on 14 April, no movement of ice cream took place from HAP's plants to any of the HD-LL stores. On 14 April, Prime Minister Modi announced a second lockdown, which was to last till 3 May. The company could, hence, not undertake any production during this phase as well. The only consolation was a Union Home Ministry communication to states, dated 12 April, permitting free movement of all trucks carrying goods (whether 'essential' or otherwise) from factory warehouses and cold storages. That made it possible for the already-produced ice cream lying at HAP's cold stores, both in and outside the plants, to be taken to the HD-LL outlets for further distribution. Actual production could resume only from 8 May at Nallur and from 10 May at Karumapuram. The Noyyal ready-to-eat plant reopened on 21 May, while it was decided to shutter the Guduvanchery facility permanently.

The effects of losing peak season business weren't small. HAP's net sales for April–June, at Rs 1,279.28 crore, were 10.1 per cent below the Rs 1,423.22 crore for the corresponding period of 2019–20. Never before had it posted negative year-on-year growth.

The culprit was ice cream sales, which fell 57.5 per cent by value in April–June 2020 over April–June 2019. For a company that had started off with ice cream, this was indeed a cold blow! Sales growth for this segment continued to be negative in the subsequent July–September 2020 quarter: minus 46.6 per cent year-on-year in July, minus 28.3 per cent in August and minus 1.1 per cent in September. Although concerns over ice cream causing COVID-19 had receded by now, state-level lockdowns were strictly enforced till July and beyond—particularly in Chennai, Madurai, Salem, Erode and other major cities/towns in Tamil Nadu. With markets not being allowed to open fully and highly restricted store entry timings, growth could return to positive territory only from October.

Protecting stakeholders

Thankfully, the milk business didn't suffer that much. The Prime Minister's 24 March lockdown address was delivered at 8.00 p.m. By around 10.00 p.m., the Home Ministry had come out with guidelines, which, among other things, listed the establishments and activities that were exempted from the blanket containment measures. These included 'manufacturing units of essential commodities,' 'dairy and milk booths,' and 'animal fodder'. In other words, barring ice cream and pizza/ready-to-eat, all of HAP's units could operate. Nothing stopped the Palani and Sangola cattle feed factories, or even the milk powder (but not ice cream) plant at Karumapuram, from running.

Sathyan had, by this time, formed a core team that worked in close coordination through a WhatsApp group. Apart from Sathyan, it had Ulhas Vasant Ambre (Associate Vice President-Plant Operations), J. Shanmuga Priyan (Associate Vice President-Internal Audit & Process Improvement), J. Jerome (Vice President-Sales), A. Sam Joseph (Senior General Manager-Sourcing & Animal Husbandry), P. Varadharaj

(General Manager-Material Management & Inbound Logistics) and K. Balashanmugam (Deputy General Manager-Outbound Logistics). The forty-eight-year-old Ambre, who was based at Salem and in charge of all HAP plants, tragically succumbed to COVID-19 on 6 August. He was the only employee—a true corona warrior—whom the company lost during the pandemic.

It was clear from the outset that milk procurement was going to be least hit by the lockdown. The Hatsun Milk Banks (HMB), being in rural areas where COVID was less of an issue, would function normally. But this wasn't so with sales. With hotels, tea shops and canteens shut, no marriages and other social functions taking place, and provision stores opening for only a few hours, demand for even milk and curd had fallen. Despite exemption from the lockdown, HAP's sales of these two fresh products, too, were nearly a fifth lower year-on-year till around 10 April. While HAP's dependence on institutional sales was far less relative to its competitors, the demand side couldn't be ignored. It was, therefore, necessary to carefully manage procurement. While February to May was generally the lean season for production, there was no need to 'chase' milk this time around. The timing of the lockdown actually worked as a blessing of sorts; had it come in July or later, handling the extra supply of milk, on top of a demand collapse, would have posed real problems.

A key decision that the HAP management took was not to recruit new farmer-suppliers. Existing farmers, however, would neither face any milk refusal nor delayed payments. Farmers, for the first time, were graded into three categories. At the top ('3-Star') were the ones who had been pouring regularly in the last 300 days and more. The bottom ('1-Star') comprised recent entrants who had joined in March before or immediately after lockdown when the new categorisation was still to be implemented. This lot was previously supplying to other dairies that had stopped buying, when demand for milk powder and ghee and from B2B consumers crashed. In between the two were the '2-Star' farmers. They were pouring before—many even in the last 150–200 days—but not regularly. 3-Star farmers were subjected to a minimal cut in procurement prices. In normal years, these would have risen during the lean summer months. Under the new abnormal circumstances, the company made sure its loyal suppliers were paid at least the rates they would have got in the flush winter season. During April–July 2020, 3-Star farmers received Rs 3–4 per litre more than 1-Star and Rs 1–2/litre over 2-Star suppliers. By December 2020, the price gap between even 3-Star and 1-Star had reduced to below Rs 1/litre.

Proof of how HAP treated its farmers in the most adverse conditions of demand destruction can be gleaned from procurement data. During April–June 2020, the worst lockdown quarter, the company's milk procurement stood merely 0.4 per cent lower than for the same period of the previous year. The following two quarters registered positive year-on-year growth rates of 9.8 per cent and 3.9 per cent, respectively. Not only were there no milk refusals, leave alone payment defaults or delays, HAP's farmers suffered no heavy price cuts, and loyalty was reasonably rewarded.

But it wasn't the farmers alone. The interests of other stakeholders, especially the employees and the franchisees were equally protected.

HAP's operations fell largely outside the lockdown's purview, being in an industry producing and delivering 'essential goods'. On 24 March night, Sathyan was on a conference call with his core team till 2.30 a.m. By 6.00 a.m., they were at the company's corporate office in Karapakkam on the Old Mahabalipuram Road, where fifteen or so other employees had also reached. The first job was to issue new identity cards clearly displaying the 'Arokya' milk brand. The existing cards of employees merely mentioned 'HAP,' which was unlikely to pass muster with the enforcement authorities. Plant heads were explicitly told to contact their local police stations in this regard. The transporters and HD franchisees had also to be given letters for ensuring free flow of milk, curd and raw material into, from and outside the plants. The company further started manufacturing surface and hand sanitizers from Karumapuram, Thalaivasal, Palacode and Hyderabad to supply to its various factories as well as the HMBs and HDs. Production of these sanitizers—mainly from diluted peracetic acid, isopropyl alcohol and other antimicrobial/disinfectant agents used in its dairies—rose to 4,000–5,000 litres per day during 1–15 April. That was when commercial sanitizers weren't available in sufficient quantities, and in-house solutions had to be trusted.

HAP's 10,500 employees included roughly 5,500 who were on fixed-term contracts. Of the latter, more than 800 were migrant workers from Bihar, Uttar Pradesh and other states. The shutdown of the ice cream and ready-to-eat plants resulted in some 600 labourers—mostly doing packing, loading and unloading work—being rendered redundant. They were all retained and their full contracted salaries paid. Some of the idle contract staff at the Karumapuram ice cream facility was redeployed for preparing sanitizers and filling these in bottles. In addition to the non-permanent employees directly engaged by the company, close to 300 workers at the Shirashi and Govindpur Thanda plant sites saw no construction activity till 14 June and 23 June, respectively. Their food and housing requirement, too, was taken care of by the contractors concerned, on the back of HAP's commitment to recommence work the moment clearances were accorded. All this made sense, both from a humanitarian as well as commercial standpoint. The lockdown was going to be a temporary affair. Once it got lifted, getting back labour wouldn't be easy. Since recruitment and training involved additional expenses and time, it wasn't worth throwing out people just to save a couple of months' costs.

During the lockdown period, the company introduced an 'essential service allowance' for all employees who were working at its plants and offices or going to the field. This daily prorated allowance, implemented between 23 March and mid-May, ranged from Rs 2,000–3,500 per month for outsourced contract labour and security staff to Rs 5,000–6,000 for team members, Rs 7,000–10,000 for managers and Rs 12,000 for senior managers. Those working exclusively from homes—they hardly numbered 650, as the bulk of employees were in production, procurement, sales and marketing that required them to be in the field for at least a few hours daily—had to take 20–40 per cent compensation reductions.

Sathyan himself began travelling and visiting the company's plants from 28–29 March. 'I would leave at about 5.00 a.m. wearing an Arokya T-shirt. My car, too, had an Arokya banner to make it easy to go past the police and border check-posts. As the roads were absolutely empty, it was possible to go to Palacode, Salem, Thalaivasal or Chittoor and return by 7.00 or 8.00 p.m.,' he says. The purpose of his going was more to set a personal example and send out a signal that, for HAP, it was business as usual. The essential service allowance for working under difficult conditions, combined with salary cuts for those opting entirely to work from home, was consistent with this approach.

There were 2,980 Hatsun Daily stores as of 31 March 2020. Out of these, 2,447 were HD-Fresh and the balance 533 HD-LL outlets. As distributors of ice cream (including to HD-Fresh stores), the HD-LL franchisees were the hardest hit by the lockdown, as they lost out on the peak demand season. P. Varadharajan of Sri Saraswathi Agencies, a franchisee at Madipakkam in south Chennai, couldn't open his store for three days till 27 March. Even after restarting, most of the ninety-odd provision shops, supermarkets and fruit and vegetable vendors in the area to which it supplied 'Arun' ice cream remained shut. Varadharajan's HD-LL store did just Rs 5.30 lakh of ice cream business in April 2020, as against Rs 29.57 lakh in April 2019.

That was where HAP stepped in. Post lockdown, the HD-LL stores were made to put up 'Arokya' milk banners or boards in order to push their retail counter sales of fresh products. They were further permitted to lift milk, curd or *paneer* directly from the company, instead of the nearby HD-Fresh outlet. In the process, the HD-LL franchisee could earn an extra margin previously accruing to the HD-Fresh store. Varadharajan's value of fresh product counter sales was only Rs 4.05 lakh in April 2019. That more than trebled to Rs 12.44 lakh in April 2020; he also enjoyed a higher margin than before. 'During the lockdown, we survived only due to Arokya milk and curd. Even by running from 6.00 am to 12.00 p.m., our sales were higher simply because the regular retail shops had shut. Also, the company was continuously supplying from its end, while the other brands were less visible,' he points out.

Keeping the distribution chain going was crucial when demand returned with the gradual lifting of lockdown restrictions. In November 2019, HAP had started rebranding its HD stores as 'HAP Daily' outlets. The same month, it launched ice cream cakes, followed by chocolates, under the 'HAP' brand. 'HAP' ice cream cake, chocolate and *kulfi* (traditional Indian ice cream) became a parallel brand to the more premium 'Ibaco' products. Like the latter, these could only be retailed through the company's outlets. With the lockdown, the focus of the HAP Daily/HD stores had to shift to milk and curd necessarily. But from July 2020, sales of 'HAP' products also started picking up, generating more business to the franchisees. The strength of the company's distribution and milk procurement networks meant that there was no dearth of supply to cater to the revived demand. That was something the competitors couldn't do as effectively. Even with regard to the 170 'Ibaco' and 216 'Oyalo' franchisees, HAP continued paying the rent and electricity for their stores— plus the monthly QSC (quality, service, cleanliness) incentive to cover basic salary and maintenance expenses—throughout the lockdown period.

Crisis to opportunity

In spite of it being the year of the lockdown, 2020–21 turned out to be one of HAP's best, given the most trying circumstances. The company ended the financial year with net sales of Rs 5,569.74 crore, a 4.9 per cent increase over the Rs 5,308.33 crore for 2019–20. This, after registering a 10.1 per cent negative sales growth—the first-ever in its history—during the April–June quarter! Further, it posted an all-time-high profit after tax of Rs 246.35 crore, more than double the preceding fiscal's Rs 112.27 crore.

More than anything else, the above numbers were a confirmation of the company's core strength, which, according to Chandramogan, lay in 'managing crises and seeing these as opening opportunities for the future'. He cites at least three previous instances where this was borne out. The first one was back in November 1985, when torrential rains washed away the railway bridge at Madurantakam connecting Chennai to coastal and southern Tamil Nadu. The bridge's repair took five or six months, during which time 'Arun' ice cream couldn't be loaded from the Egmore railway station. Instead, it had to be dispatched from the Tollgate plant to the Katpadi station that was 150 km westwards. Transporting and booking trains from Katpadi entailed additional cost, 'but we chose to bear it because much of our sales were in the southern, eastern and central districts'.

In 2002–03, there was a shortage of dry ice due to an erratic supply of carbon dioxide gas by fertilizer plants. The company, then, resorted to importing dry ice in container ships and even air-lifting a few consignments from Singapore. This time, too, the higher cost wasn't passed on to consumers, 'as our priority was to maintain supply and loyalty'. The final occasion came after the Great Tsunami of 26 December 2004. HAP's distributors and employees went the extra mile in delivering 'Arokya' milk to the worst-affected areas of Nagapattinam and Cuddalore, where even vehicles couldn't go beyond a point. 'We are used to taking extraordinary efforts in any crisis. The lockdown was arguably the worst, but it again brought out the best in us,' points out Chandramogan.

In all crises, the focus has been on ensuring the reliability of supply and continuity of operations to consumers, franchisees, farmers and vendors, even if it means losing money in the short run. HAP's milk procurement averaged a record 29.01 lakh litres per day in 2020–21, 6.4 per cent more than the 27.26 lakh litres of last fiscal, along with a rise in the number of farmer-suppliers from 3.81 lakh to 4.14 lakh. The company continued buying from farmers, unlike many private and even cooperative dairies that slashed purchases the moment they saw demand contracting and stocks building up. HAP didn't desert its farmers, knowing from past experience how such short-termism never pays.

The same goes for the distribution network. As of 31 March 2021, the company had a total of 3,612 outlets, comprising 2,718 HAP Daily-Fresh, 569 HAP Daily-LL, 155 Ibaco and 170 Oyalo stores. That made it also the owner of India's largest network of retail brand stores, spread across Tamil Nadu, Pondicherry, Andhra Pradesh, Telangana, Kerala, Karnataka, Goa, Maharashtra, Gujarat, Chhattisgarh and Odisha.

The HAP Daily/HD outlets were launched to supply to provision shops, supermarkets, departmental stores and restaurants, with only 10–15 per cent of sales being to retail consumers. But their counter sales grew by over 50 per cent during 2020–21 post the lockdown. Since milk and curd weren't available in regular stores— most of them had shut or operated only for a few hours—more consumers started coming to the HAP Daily outlets. As footfalls rose, the company not only made sure that they were adequately stocked with 'Arokya' milk, 'Arun' ice cream or 'Hatsun' curd, but also rolled out new products such as ice cream cake, chocolates and *kulfi* under the 'HAP' brand. The latter products were not for redistribution and only for exclusive retailing through the HAP Daily outlets, like 'Ibaco' ice cream and 'Oyalo' pizza.

Seamless product availability and distribution is what really helped when the economy started unlocking. The consumers who bought 'Arokya' milk and 'Hatsun' curd, especially from HAP Daily stores, did not switch to other brands even after the lockdown was over. Even ice cream sales, which had plunged 57.5 per cent year-on-year in April–June and 26.2 per cent in July–September, grew 19 per cent in the third quarter. And by the last quarter, all cylinders were firing: not only did the company's net sales go up 23.9 per cent, the growth in the case of ice cream for January–March 2021 over January–March 2020 was close to 69 per cent.

'We have all along sought to build economic moats against competition—whether through buying milk directly from farmers and providing them quality cattle feed and animal husbandry services or investing in our brands, processing, cold chain and distribution infrastructure. These have delivered us returns in terms of gaining market share and protecting margins,' says Chandramogan.

The same moats delivered in 2020–21, converting a crisis year into one that opened new opportunities.